MORE STORYTIME MAGIC

ALA Editions purchases fund advocacy,
awareness, and accreditation programs
for library professionals worldwide.

MORE STORYTIME MAGIC

Kathy MacMillan and

Christine Kirker

with illustrations by Melanie Fitz

AMERICAN LIBRARY ASSOCIATION

Chicago   2016

Kathy MacMillan and Christine Kirker are the coauthors of four previous volumes in the Storytime Magic series from ALA Editions: *Storytime Magic* (2009), *Kindergarten Magic* (2011), *Multicultural Storytime Magic* (2012), and *Baby Storytime Magic* (2014). They also share storytime resources at their website, www.storytimestuff.net.

KATHY MacMILLAN is a writer, American Sign Language interpreter, and storyteller. She is the author of *Try Your Hand at This! Easy Ways to Incorporate Sign Language into Your Programs* (Scarecrow Press, 2006), *A Box Full of Tales* (ALA Editions, 2008), and *Little Hands and Big Hands: Children and Adults Signing Together* (Huron Street Press, 2013), as well as a young adult novel, *Sword and Verse* (HarperCollins, 2016). She has worked in school and public libraries since 1997, specializing in programming for all ages. She holds a Master of Library Science degree from the University of Maryland, College Park, and reviewed for *School Library Journal* for sixteen years. She presents American Sign Language programs and resources at www.storiesbyhand.com.

CHRISTINE KIRKER is a library associate with the Carroll County (Maryland) Public Library. Since joining the library staff in 2005, Christine has developed and presented many programs for children of all ages, including monthly preschool science programs. In addition, she has applied for, and been awarded, a variety of grants that have supported a wide range of programming for the library. Previously, Christine spent ten years at the University of Maryland, Baltimore County (UMBC), as a research analyst for the Office of Institutional Research.

© 2016 by the American Library Association

Illustrations by Melanie Fitz and Christine Kirker

The American Sign Language (ASL) graphic images in this book have been provided by the Institute for Disabilities Research and Training, Inc. through their online software, myASLTech.com.

While we have made every effort to provide accurate pronunciation guides for the foreign language materials in this book, we acknowledge that, due to the dynamic nature of language across settings and regions, pronunciations by native users may vary.

Extensive effort has gone into ensuring the reliability of the information in this book; however, the publisher makes no warranty, express or implied, with respect to the material contained herein.

ISBN: 978-0-8389-1368-0 (paper).

Library of Congress Cataloging-in-Publication Data

Names: MacMillan, Kathy, 1975– author. | Kirker, Christine, author.
Title: More storytime magic / Kathy MacMillan and Christine Kirker ; with illustrations by Melanie Fitz.
Description: Chicago : ALA Editions, an imprint of the American Library Association, 2016. | Includes bibliographical references and index.
Identifiers: LCCN 2015028691 | ISBN 9780838913680 (print : alk. paper)
Subjects: LCSH: Children's libraries—Activity programs—United States. | Storytelling—United States.
Classification: LCC Z718.3 .M2524 2016 | DDC 027.62/51--dc23 LC record available at http://lccn.loc .gov/2015028691

Cover design by Kirstin Krutsch. Image © Lorelyn Medina/Shutterstock, Inc.

Book design by Karen Sheets de Gracia in Candy Randy, Kristen ITC, Georgia, and Helvetica. Composition by Dianne M. Rooney.

♾ This paper meets the requirements of ANSI/NISO Z39.48–1992 (Permanence of Paper).

Printed in the United States of America

20 19 18 17 16   5 4 3 2 1

*For every child who ever giggled at one
of my silly storytime jokes.*

—KM

*For my dearest friends who have endured
my humor for so many years.
Thanks for your love and support!*

—CMK

Contents

WEB **Flannelboard patterns, craft patterns, and worksheets are available online at alaeditions.org/webextras.**

Acknowledgments

THANK YOU TO the many people who made this project possible, especially Jamie Santoro and the team at ALA Editions; JX MacMillan, who contributed many ideas to this book; Corinne Vinopol and Alex Leffers at the Institute for Disabilities Research and Training, Inc.; Melanie Fitz; and the many workshop participants and newsletter contributors who have inspired us with their enthusiasm and ideas.

1

Keeping the Magic in Storytime

Principles of Engagement in Storytimes

Engaging storytime audiences really means catching and holding the attention of kids and parents. The techniques for doing so vary widely from group to group and depend on the ages of the children, their familiarity with storytime, the tone set by the presenter, group dynamics, and sometimes just the vibe in the room. The best storytime presenters are the most flexible—the better you are at reading your group and adapting materials on the fly, the more likely you are to keep children and adults engaged throughout the program.

The good news is that there are some tried-and-true approaches that will help engage children at storytime! Here are a few indispensable tips:

- ▶ Plan to use a variety of formats: books, flannelboards, storyboards, puppets, storytelling, perhaps even videos.

- ▶ Make your program as participative as possible. Don't expect kids to sit and listen the whole time. Ask them questions, and make time for their answers. Invite them to act out stories, dance along with the music, or help place items on the flannelboard.

- ▶ Make sure your storytime materials represent a variety—alternate books with songs, fingerplays, bounces and tickles (for babies and toddlers), riddles (for older children), and poems.

▶ Practice! Be prepared so you don't flounder during the program. Any moment that you seem unsure what to do next is a moment when the group's attention can waver.

▶ Take care of the basics—make sure everyone can see and hear what's happening. A child who can't access the story is much more likely to lose interest and cause mischief. Prevent problems by taking a moment to handle such issues up front.

▶ Display words to songs and fingerplays whenever possible by using a whiteboard, chalkboard, printout, or projector. This practice supports word recognition for children and encourages those who can read well (older children and adults) to sing along and participate.

▶ Don't forget to introduce yourself at the beginning of the program! This is a small detail, but it will help children and parents feel welcome.

▶ Use music to set the mood. Play upbeat music as children enter the storytime area. If the group gets wild, play calming music. Play "winding down" music during cleanup time. (One of our favorite not-so-subtle musical hints is playing "Happy Trails" when it's time to exit the room!)

▶ Plan to present the material that requires the most sustained attention at the beginning of the program, when children are fresh. Save any loud or large-movement activities (such as the parachute activity in chapter 11) for the end, as it can be difficult to regain the group's focus afterward.

▶ No matter how well you have planned your program, stuff happens. Always be prepared with alternatives should your group be younger than expected, have difficulty settling, or be more sedate than expected.

▶ Alternate large-movement activities with sitting-down times, so that you do not tax children's attention spans too much.

▶ Engage parents whenever possible, so that they don't sit in the back and chatter. One way to involve parents is to solicit the kids' help. For example, you might say, "Kids, let's all make sure our grown-ups brought their happy faces. Did they? Let's see them!"

▶ Encourage children to make name tags before the program. Use their names whenever possible. If your group size allows, sing a hello song that incorporates each child's name. If a child is being disruptive, sometimes simply using his or her name can bring that child back into the group without incident. You might say, for example, "Daniel, what do you think the crocodile did then?"

▶ Have fun! If the children see you enjoying yourself, they will enjoy themselves, too.

Aligning with Benchmarks and Standards

Various standards and benchmarks have been a part of the education world for years, with many states recently adopting the Common Core State Standards, which identify the reading, writing, and mathematics skills that students should develop at each grade level. Though there has been controversy about the expectations of the standards, particularly among early childhood educators, the fact is that teachers, students, and parents all over the country are being affected by the implementation of these standards. If libraries want to remain relevant, they need to provide resources that align with those the schools are using. In some cases, the decision about whether to fund a library initiative may even come down to how clearly its supporters can articulate the library's alignment with the Common Core.

The good news is that you probably already are doing lots of things in your storytimes that support the aims of the Common Core—the trick is to learn how to speak the language of the standards so that educators, administrators, board members, and lawmakers can understand how storytime contributes to those standards.

In *More Storytime Magic*, we have tried to make it easier to align your programs with the Common Core by coding each entry to indicate which of the standards that activity supports. For example, *IIA1* refers to the listing of the standards in appendix B:

II. Mathematics

    A. Counting and Cardinality

        1. Count to 100 by ones and by tens.

The standards listed in appendix B focus on the skills a child is expected to develop by the *end* of kindergarten. In coding the activities in this book, we have highlighted the skills each activity supports, with the recognition that preschoolers are still developing language and numerical literacy. Therefore, any counting activity, for example, would support a child's development toward the standard just cited. Early childhood educators and librarians have long recognized that early literacy does not mean the ability to read; rather, early literacy involves the constellation of skills, such as letter knowledge, vocabulary, and understanding of print conventions, that support later reading and writing. Similarly, we must approach the standards with the understanding that they are simply targets and that the stories, songs, rhymes, and activities we use in storytime support the broader language and mathematics skills children will be expected to master later in kindergarten. Many of our storytime materials already do this by encouraging children to compare sizes, classify, use language to describe qualities of objects, and use mathematical vocabulary. Aligning your programs with the standards does not necessarily mean doing anything differently but, rather, learning to describe your storytime activities in the language of benchmarks.

See appendix B for a complete listing of the standards.

Making Storytimes Accessible to All

The mission of the public library includes service to all, and that in itself should mean libraries provide accommodations upon request. But such accommodations are also required by law in the United States; under Title II of the Americans with Disabilities Act, public entities such as libraries are required to provide accommodations upon request to people with disabilities. This requirement may mean adapting your program plan, or providing an alternate entry for people with mobility impairments, or providing sensory-friendly storytimes with lower volume and less visual stimulation for children on the autism spectrum. Perhaps the most common accommodation requested for storytimes is an American Sign Language interpreter.

Despite the fact that accommodations are required by law, many libraries are shockingly unprepared to respond to requests for interpreters or other accommodations. It is vital that all public services staff know what to do when a request comes in and that costs for accommodations are incorporated into the library's budget at the highest level. Accommodations should be viewed not as "extra" services but, rather, as the cost of making the library's services available to the entire community. All program publicity should include a note about accessibility, with clear instructions and contact information for requesting accommodations.

All children in storytime benefit from the provision of accommodations, whether they are using those accommodations directly or not. The presenter's attitude is vital to setting the tone for inclusion and respect for diversity. The techniques for engagement listed earlier in this chapter are often even more necessary when children with special needs are in attendance.

Ask the child's parent what accommodations may need to be made in order for the child to get the most out of storytime. Accommodations may include the following:

Placement. Location is particularly important for children who are deaf or hard of hearing—they should be seated near the front of the room for the best sightlines. The interpreter should be as close to the presenter as possible, so that the children can follow both. For children with mobility issues, find a place that is easy to get to and will allow for maximum participation.

Getting and keeping children's attention. Some children with special needs—and some without special needs, too!—may find it difficult to transfer their attention from one task to another. Getting children's attention may be as simple as using a visual signal, flickering the lights, singing a certain song, or repeating a special verse. These sorts of rituals provide comfort for all children, but they are particularly important in helping children with special needs make sense of their world.

Assessing understanding. Adults typically assess children's understanding by asking questions. When working with children with special needs, you may need to allow additional time for children to process your questions before answering. Because of differences in learning styles, allowing an extra moment before calling on someone to answer can level the playing field for typically developing children as well. Some children naturally take more time to process than others. Another simple, effective way to assess your group's understanding is to ask a question and have all the children respond simultaneously using a sign or gesture. For example, you might say, "If you think the fox will try to eat the grapes, touch your nose. If you think the fox will run away, touch your belly button." Structuring questions in this way also offers equal access to students who communicate through an interpreter, as the interpreting of your message necessarily means the deaf child will get it slightly later than his or her hearing peers.

Turn-taking. Many children with special needs respond well to visual or tactile prompts, so consider using a "talking stick," stuffed animal, or other special object that denotes whose turn it is to speak.

Placement of props and materials. You may need to keep materials out of reach or even out of sight until needed. Children on the autism spectrum may become easily overstimulated or distracted. Keep your storytime area uncluttered to maximize their focus.

Mobility. Throughout this book, we have included many movement activities. Young children learn best when their senses are engaged, and movement is a valuable way to engage them. However, if you have a child with limited mobility in your storytime, consider choosing movement activities for the entire group based on what that child can do, so that he or she is not left out.

In essence, every child is an individual with special needs. Looking at your storytime with this attitude means that you accept and include each child. *Attitude* is the most important factor in working with children with special needs. Remember that, even if a child is behind peers cognitively, that child is absorbing language and information about the world through interactions with you and other children. Caring and inclusive experiences lay the foundation for self-esteem and further academic development.

When in doubt, remember—focus on what a child *can* do, rather than what he or she cannot do.

The activities in this book are recommended for storytimes for ages 2 and up. Entries especially appropriate for toddler storytimes are starred.

2

All About Me

My Body

1 All About Me

I have two eyes so I can see, *(point to eyes)*
And a nose to smell things around me. *(point to nose)*
My mouth can eat tasty treats, *(point to mouth)*
And my ears hear when my mom calls, "No more sweets!" *(point to ears)*

     IC2, IE5

2 *Bandage Song (to the tune of "My Darling Clementine")

Pass out colorful stick-on bandages (or paper cutouts of bandages) and encourage the children to place the bandages on the body parts mentioned in the song.

I've got a bandage, got a bandage
Got a bandage on my nose.
I've got a cut so I need a bandage,
Need a bandage on my nose.

. . . on my leg
. . . on my tummy
. . . on my knee
. . . on my foot
. . . on my arm
. . . on my ear

    IC2, IE5

3 *Feet

Act out the words as you say the rhyme.

Feet can kick and feet can stomp.
Feet can run and feet can tromp.
Feet can walk and turn around.
Feet can be still and make no sound.

    IC2, IE5

4 *Fingers

Open fingers, close them tight, *(hold hands open, then make fists)*
Wiggle them out of sight. *(wiggle fingers and move behind your back)*
Raise those fingers way up high, *(raise hands above head)*
Now wave them slowly side to side. *(wave hands side to side)*
Hold them open, curl them closed, *(hold hands open, palms up, then curl fingers closed)*
Tap them gently on your nose. *(tap nose with both hands)*
Lace your fingers tight together, *(lace fingers together)*
Now drift them down like floating feathers. *(wiggle fingers in a downward motion)*
Fingers shake and fingers clap, *(shake hands, clap hands)*
Now fold them gently in your lap. *(fold hands in lap)*

    IC2, IE5

5 *Hands

Happy hands go clap clap clap. *(clap hands)*
Nervous hands go tap tap tap. *(tap fingers on leg)*
Gentle hands move slow, slow, slow. *(move hands gently as if petting an animal)*
Proud hands say "Way to go!" *(wave hands in air)*

    IC2, IE5

6 ***I Have Two**

I have two feet, *(point to feet)*
I have two eyes, *(point to eyes)*
I have two hands to wave up high. *(wave hands)*
I have two legs, *(point to legs)*
But just one nose, *(point to nose)*
I guess I only need one of those. *(shrug)*

> **IC2, IE5**

7 **Salon Days** (to the tune of "Here We Go 'Round the Mulberry Bush")

Mime the actions in each verse as you sing the song.

This is the way my hair is washed,
Hair is washed, hair is washed,
This is the way my hair is washed,
Water, shampoo, suds!

This is the way my hair is cut,
Hair is cut, hair is cut,
This is the way my hair is cut,
Chop, snip, snap!

This is the way my hair is dried,
Hair is dried, hair is dried,
This is the way my hair is dried,
Vroom, zoom, blow!

This is the way my hair is styled,
Hair is styled, hair is styled,
This is the way my hair is styled,
Comb, brush, go!

> **IC2, IE4, IE5**

8 ***Spider Crawl**

Pass out pom-poms to use as spiders, or use your bent fingers to represent the spider crawling.

The spider's crawling on my leg,
Where will he go?
There is no use in asking me—
Only the spider knows! *(jump the spider to a different body part)*

Now the spider's on my _____ *(let children identify body part)*
Where will he go?
There is no use in asking me—
Only the spider knows! *(repeat, jumping spider to other body parts)*

> **IC2, IE5**

9 T-E-E-T-H Flannelboard/Magnetboard (to the tune of "B-I-N-G-O")

Discuss proper tooth care and demonstrate how brushing removes plaque from teeth. Place the teeth on the board with the letters over the teeth. As you sing the song, use a toothbrush to "brush" a letter away before each verse.

I always take care of my teeth,
I brush them every day.
T-E-E-T-H,
T-E-E-T-H,
T-E-E-T-H,
I brush the plaque away.

Continue, gradually replacing letters with brushing sounds, until you have brushed away all the letters.

IC2, IC3, IE5

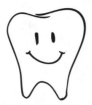 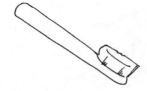 

More Entries Related to This Topic

Feelings

10 *Are You Happy? (to the tune of "Frère Jacques")

Act out the facial expressions and actions in each verse as you sing the song.

Are you happy? Are you happy?
Yes, I am. Yes, I am.
I'm smiling 'cause I'm happy,
Clapping 'cause I'm happy.
Yes, I am. Yes, I am.

Are you sad? . . . frowning . . . crying . . .
Are you angry? . . . stomping . . . grumbling . . .
Are you frightened? . . . shivering . . . hiding . . .
Are you excited? . . . bouncing . . . grinning . . .

IE5, IE6

11 A Balloon's Tale: A Prop Story

Items needed: balloon, pen, puppet or stuffed animal

Preparation: Draw a smiley face on a balloon. You may wish to inflate and then deflate the balloon ahead of time, so that it will be easier to blow up during the story.

Once upon a time, there was a little balloon. *(hold up deflated balloon)*
He was so excited about his first day of school that he danced all around.
　　(make balloon wiggle)
When he got to school, he met his teacher, who was so nice. It made him feel so
　　grown-up to go to school. *(blow up balloon a little)*
Then he made some new friends! *(hold up puppet)*
That was so much fun that it filled him up even more. *(blow up balloon a little more)*
Then it was time for recess! He loved that. It made his smile grow so big! *(blow up
　　balloon even more)*
He got to play on the swings and the slide, and his friends said, "We like you!" That
　　made him feel great! Like he was full of smiles! *(blow up balloon even more)*
But then . . . then one of his friends said something not very nice, and do you know
　　how that little balloon felt? *(let the air out of the balloon)*
He felt like all the good thoughts had gone out of him. His smile went away. The little
　　balloon felt empty. His teacher saw how he was feeling, and she had a talk with
　　the class about words. "Some words can hurt people and make them feel like all
　　the good thoughts have gone out of them," she said. The little balloon nodded.
　　(make balloon nod)
That was exactly how he felt.
"But," said his teacher, "some words can make us feel like we are getting filled up
　　again with good things." She looked right at the balloon's friend. "Can you think
　　of any of those words?"
"Sorry," he whispered.
The little balloon started to feel a tiny bit better. *(blow up balloon a little bit)*
The teacher went on. "Can you think of more good words that help people feel
　　better?" she asked. *(invite the children to suggest words; if desired, write the
　　words on a board to reinforce reading and spelling skills)*
Then the teacher said, "One of my favorite words is 'love.' It's the kind of word that
　　gets bigger the more we share it!" *(write love on the back of the balloon and
　　then blow it up)*
The little balloon saw that she was right! The word got bigger and bigger as his smile
　　grew. *(tie a knot into the end of the balloon)*
"Come on, friends!" he said. "Let's play!"

Play a tossing game with the balloon. Ask each child to share a happy word each time the balloon comes to him or her.

It's a good idea to have a backup balloon ready in case the one you are using pops! If this happens, say, "And then he almost exploded with happiness!" Then take out the second balloon and resume the story.

IE1, IE5, IE6

12 Bear Is Sad: A Participation Story

Use a stuffed bear or puppet as the main character of this story.

My friend Bear is sad today. How can you tell when someone is sad? *(take answers from the children and show how Bear is doing those things; possible answers: frowning, crying, slumped shoulders, sighing, not interested in playing)*

What could we do to cheer Bear up? I know! Let's sing a song! What song should we sing? *(take suggestions from children, then select a song and have everyone sing it together)*

There! Now do you feel better, Bear? *(make Bear shake head)*

Oh no! He's still not feeling better. What else could we do to cheer Bear up? *(take suggestions from the children, but if anyone suggests a hug or kiss, act doubtful; if needed, guide children with the following suggestions):*

▶ Tickle him *(let each child tickle the bear)*

▶ Tell him a joke *(select a child to tell a joke or tell one of your own)*

▶ Dance *(put on some music and have everyone dance)*

▶ Jump up and down

▶ Play peek-a-boo

▶ Have a snack *(eat pretend cookies)*

After each attempt, ask Bear if he feels better and have him shake his head.

I don't know, Bear, we have tried so many ways to cheer you up, but you are still sad. Can you all help me remember the different ways we tried to cheer Bear up? *(with input from the children, list the activities in order; use words like "first, second, then, next" to emphasize sequencing)*

What else could we possibly do to cheer Bear up? *(if any of the children says "hug" or "kiss," seize on that suggestion; if not, have Bear whisper in your ear)*

A hug? A kiss? I guess it's worth a try. *(have each child give the bear a hug and a kiss)*

Do you feel happier now, Bear? *(make Bear nod head)*

It worked! He feels happy! How can you tell when someone is happy? *(guide suggestions if necessary: smiling, laughing, bouncing, wants to play)*

Thank you for helping to cheer Bear up! Yay!

IE1, IE5, IE6

More Entries Related to This Topic

Senses

13 *Night Owl Flannelboard and Sound Story

Based on the book by Toni Yuly (New York: Macmillan, 2015)

Night Owl listens to the sounds of the night, waiting for his very favorite one: his mother returning home! As you tell the story, play clips of the sounds that Night Owl hears and ask the children to identify them. You can find a collection of sound clips to download for the story at www.storytimestuff.net.

IC2

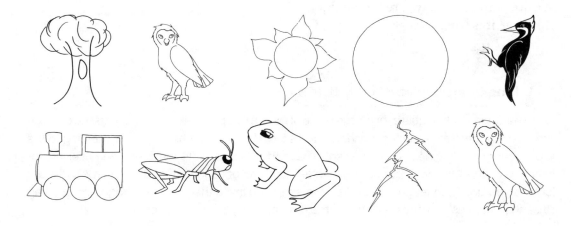

14 Senses Song (to the tune of "My Darling Clementine")

Begin by inviting the children to list things they can smell. Write their suggestions on a whiteboard, chalkboard, or flipchart paper and use them in the second verse of the song.

I've got a nose, got a nose,
Got a nose right here. (point to nose)
And my nose is how I smell,
Got a nose right here.

With my nose, I smell _____,
I smell _____, I smell _____,
With my nose, I smell _____,
I smell _____, I smell _____,

Repeat the activity with other senses:

I've got eyes . . . and my eyes are how I see . . .
I've got ears . . . and my ears are how I hear . . .

I've got a tongue . . . and my tongue is how I taste . . .
I've got fingers . . . and my fingers help me touch . . .

IC2, ID2, IE1, IE5

Another Entry Related to This Topic

Transportation Sounds Game, p. 164

We Are All Different

15 I Am Special (to the tune of "Frère Jacques")

I am special, I am special,
So are you, so are you.
We are both unique, we are both unique,
It is true, it is true!

IC2

16 Liking Song (to the tune of "Good Night Ladies")

On a whiteboard, chalkboard, or a large piece of flipchart paper, make a list of things the children like, such as ice cream, kittens, baseball, and so on. Invite each child to add something to the list. If your group is older, you may wish to have the children write their items themselves, for writing practice. With younger children, write the name of each item on the list, spelling it out loud as you go. Then teach the children the song and invite them to sing it together, pointing to each person as you say his or her name, and pointing to the items on the list.

Katie likes kittens.
Bobby likes reading.
Tara likes bowling.
River likes hot dogs.

Before you sing each verse, review the children's names and the words on the list that will be in the song. If you need extra items to fill out the final verse, add yourself or items that everyone likes, such as "storytime" and "the library." For example:

Jenny likes porcupines.
Miss Kathy likes trains.
We all like the library.
We all like storytime!

ID2, IE1, IE5

17 What I Like

Pass out one star to each child. Then place the ice cream cone, cookie, and pretzel on the flannelboard. Invite each child to come forward and place a star next to the treat he or she would like best. Then count how many stars are next to each treat. On a whiteboard, chalkboard, or piece of flipchart paper, write the name of each treat and the number of children who voted for it. Point out that writing the word and showing a picture are different ways of showing the foods, just like the stars and writing the numbers are different ways of showing amounts. Ask questions such as the following:

▶ Which treat has the most stars?

▶ Which treat has the fewest stars?

▶ Does the ice cream have more stars than the cookie, or fewer?

Repeat the game with different kinds of drinks (milk, orange juice, water) and different kinds of toys (ball, blocks, teddy bear). Add the new items to the list and ask questions about each set as you do so. When you have finished all three sets of items, encourage the children to look at the whole list. Review the items and the numbers next to them. Ask questions about the whole list, such as the following:

▶ Which item got the most votes?

▶ Which item got the fewest votes?

▶ Did any of the items get the same number of votes?

▶ Did the orange juice get more votes than the ball, or fewer?

IIA1, IIA3, IIA4, IIA5, IIA6, IIA7

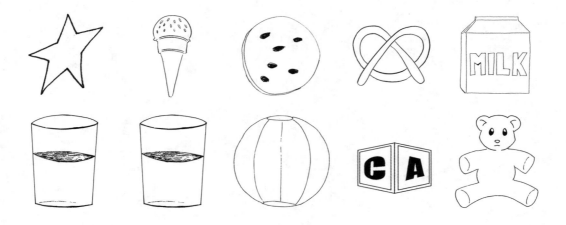

Another Entry Related to This Topic

*Apple-Dapple , p. 120

Recommended Books

Always by Emma Dodd. Somerville, MA: Templar Books, 2014.

Cheer Up, Mouse! by Jed Henry. New York: Houghton Mifflin, 2012.

Taking a Bath with the Dog and Other Things That Make Me Happy by Scott Menchin. Cambridge, MA: Candlewick, 2007.

So Many Feelings: Sign Language for Feelings and Emotions by Dawn Babb Prochovnic. Minneapolis, MN: Magic Wagon, 2012.

Birdie's Big-Girl Hair by Sujean Rim. New York: Little, Brown, 2014.

Hands Say Love by George Shannon. New York: Little, Brown, 2014.

Baby's Got the Blues by Carol Diggory Shields. Somerville, MA: Candlewick, 2014.

Can YOU Make a Scary Face? by Jan Thomas. New York: Simon and Schuster, 2009.

Bear Feels Sick by Karma Wilson. New York: McElderry Books, 2007.

In My Heart by Jo Witek. New York: Abrams, 2013.

3

Animals

18 **Animal Guessing Song** (to the tune of "It's a Small World After All")

Oh, I am long and green and I love to swim,
But if I'm in the water you can't come in.
And I swim down the Nile
With a big toothy smile.
I'm a crocodile!

Oh, I'm big and gray with a great long trunk,
And when I walk I go thunk thunk.
Can you guess who I am?
It's okay if you can't.
I'm an elephant!

Oh, I'm big and gray and I love to wade
In the nice cool water and stay in the shade.
Well, I don't want a fuss,
I'm the size of a bus.
I'm a rhinoceros!

Well, I'm long and thin and I slither around,
In the dry hot desert is where I am found.
People shiver and shake
When my rattle I shake.
I'm a rattlesnake!

IC2

19 *Chicken Cheeks* **Block Story**

Based on the book by Michael Ian Black (New York: Simon and Schuster, 2008)

A group of animals creates a tower to reach a bee's honey stash—but the bee has other ideas.

The text of this silly picture book consists of silly names for the various animals' backsides, including "moose caboose" and "penguin patootie." For a fun telling or retelling, attach the animal pictures to blocks and have the children stack them up, then knock the tower over when the bee attacks and the animals scatter.

IA3

Birds

20 The Crow and the Pitcher: An Aesop's Fable Prop Story

Items needed: a pitcher with a little bit of water in it, a crow puppet, a bag or basket of pebbles

Caw! Caw! I'm a crow! And boy, am I thirsty! I've been flying and flying. I haven't seen any water anywhere! Have you all seen any water around? *(children point out pitcher)*

Hey, you're right! There is some water in there! Thanks! *(crow tries to reach water, but can't; feel free to get really silly with this, having the crow flip over backwards, climb the side of the pitcher, get a running start, etc.)*

Oh, no! I am so thirsty! How can I get the water out? *(if someone suggests pouring the water out, have the crow pretend to try to lift the pitcher, but claim that it's too heavy)*

Oh, if only we had some pebbles. *(if children don't point out the pebbles, point them out)*

There we go, perfect! What do you think we can do with the pebbles? *(take suggestions; if no one suggests putting the pebbles in the pitcher, have the crow say:)*

What do you think will happen if we put the pebbles in the pitcher? *(discuss their guesses)* Let's try it! *(let each child drop a pebble in the pitcher)*

Look at that! The water level is rising! Now I can reach the water! *(have the crow take a very noisy drink)*

Why did the water level go up when we put the pebbles in? *(discuss what happened)*

The pebbles took up space and pushed the water up! Thanks everyone! *(have the crow take another noisy drink, then fly away)*

> **IA3, IE6, IID2**

21 *Early Bird* Flannelboard

Based on the book by Toni Yuly (New York: Macmillan, 2014)

A red bird races across the grass, through the flowerbed, and more to find the early worm—but only to enjoy breakfast with a friend.

> **IA3, IIE1**

22 I'm Hungry Flannelboard

Refrain:

Baby birds are squawking in their nest,
"I'm hungry, I'm hungry," they beg and request.
Mama Bird tweets a happy song,
"I'll be back with a juicy worm and I won't be long."
Mama flies away and returns with one worm for the first baby.
"Gulp!"

Repeat refrain until Mama Bird has fed all the baby birds.

Baby birds are all sleeping in their nest,
Mama Bird is happy to take a rest!
Just as Mama is about to snore,
All the babies wake up and squawk, "More!"

IA3, IIA1

23 Parakeet (to the tune of "Lollipop")

Parakeet, parakeet, oh para-parakeet.
Parakeet, parakeet, oh para-parakeet.
Parakeet!

Love my little parakeet,
Tell you why.
He flaps his wings and starts to fly.
And when he sings his little chirping song,
Man, I have to sing along.

I love my parakeet, parakeet, oh para-parakeet.
Parakeet, parakeet, oh para-parakeet.
Parakeet!

IC2

24 Woodpecker, Woodpecker

Begin by teaching the ASL signs TREE and BIRD. Explain that in this rhyme, you will be learning about a specific kind of bird called a woodpecker and will be using the signs to show how the woodpecker uses the tree. To see a video demonstration of these signs, visit www.storytimestuff.net.

Woodpecker, woodpecker, time to eat! *(sign BIRD)*
Woodpecker, woodpecker, fly to the tree. *(sign TREE with your other hand and move the BIRD to your forearm)*
Tap-tap-tap-tap-tap-tap-tap-tap-tap-tap-tap-tap-tap! *(make the bird's beak tap quickly on your forearm, which represents the tree trunk)*
Now eat up the bugs you found, just like that. *(move fingers to show beak eating bugs)*

Woodpecker, woodpecker, time to sleep! *(sign BIRD)*
Woodpecker, woodpecker, fly to the tree. *(sign TREE with your other hand and move the BIRD to your forearm)*
Tap-tap-tap-tap-tap-tap-tap-tap-tap-tap-tap-tap-tap! *(make the bird's beak tap quickly on your forearm, which represents the tree trunk)*
Now nestle in the hole you made, cozy as can be! *(nestle bird in palm of hand)*

IC2

bird

tree

Farm Animals and Pets

25 *Bow, Wow, Wow (adapted traditional)

Use a dog puppet to introduce this rhyme, then repeat the rhyme as you go around the circle and insert each child's name as the dog greets him or her.

Bow, wow, wow, whose dog art thou?
Little Tommy Tinker's dog, bow, wow, wow.
Bow, wow, wow, whose dog art thou?
Little _____'s dog, bow, wow, wow.

IC2

26 *Cock-a-Doodle Quack! Quack! Flannelboard

Based on the book by Ivor Baddiel and Sophie Jubb (New York: Random House, 2007)

Baby Rooster receives advice from the other farm animals on how to wake everyone up in the morning, but he figures out the best way for himself.

IA3

27 *Little Duck Action Rhyme

I have a little duck
That says quack when we play.
Little duck follows me,
With a waddle and a sway. *(waddle in place)*
Little duck, little duck,
What did you say? *(hold hand to ear)*
I love you,
Through the night and day! *(blow kisses)*

IC2

Forest and Garden Animals

28 *Black Snake

Pass out lengths of black ribbon or crepe streamers and invite the children to make their "snakes" slither along the ground as you say this rhyme.

Black snake, black snake,
Slither to and fro,
All through the garden
Where the vegetables grow.

Black snake, black snake,
Slither near and far,
All through the garden
Then to the neighbor's yard.

Black snake, black snake,
Slither around the pole,
All through the garden
Then back in your hole.

IC2

29 *The Little Mouse: A Finger Rhyme

Here comes the little mouse, *(hold one hand with fingers apart)*
Climbing up the wall *(move index finger of other hand up the thumb to show mouse
    climbing wall)*
He jumps from here to there to there *(make mouse jump from thumb to index finger
    and then to each remaining finger)*
To there and down he falls! *(make mouse slide down outside of pinky)*

   IC2

30 The Worm's House

In the book *Ned's New Home* by Kevin Tseng (Berkeley, CA: Tricycle, 2009), Ned the worm
loves living in an apple—until the apple rots and the walls turn to mush. Ned tries moving into
an assortment of other fruits, but none is just right until he finds an apple tree. Follow up with
this action rhyme that reinforces the key points of the story:

If I were a little worm, *(wiggle index finger like a worm)*
An apple would be my home. *(hold hands together to make the shape of an apple)*
But when the apple started to rot *(collapse fingers inward)*
I would have to roam. *(wiggle index finger around to show worm roaming)*
Maybe a pear could be my house. *(hold hands together with fingers apart to show
    pear shape)*
Oh no! Too wobbly! *(make pear shape wobble)*
And a watermelon just won't do—*(hold hands apart to show watermelon size)*
It's much too big for me.
I'd build a house of blueberries, *(mime stacking blueberries)*
But they would roll away. *(roll hands)*
Maybe I'll try a lemon. *(hold hands together to show lemon shape)*
No, it's much too sour every day. *(pucker lips)*
Kiwi is sweet, but much too green. *(hold hands together to show kiwi shape)*
No one can find me there, *(shade eyes with hand as if looking for something)*
So I'd try a bowl of cherries, *(hold one hand to be bowl, make index finger of other
    hand wiggle in)*
But get lifted in the air! *(lift index finger high in the air)*
It's a bird! He's carrying me high! *(make index finger fly around)*
The air's no place for me.
So down I jump, and I would land *(show index finger jumping)*
In an apple tree! *(hold other hand up to represent branches of tree, show index
    finger jumping down into it)*
An apple! That's my perfect home *(hold hands together to represent apple)*
Red and round and warm.
An apple is the perfect home
For this little worm. *(wiggle index finger)*

   IA3, IC2

31 *Slow Snail* Flannelboard

Based on the book by Mary Murphy (Somerville, MA: Candlewick, 2012)

A snail moves s-l-o-w-l-y over objects in the garden to get to the bush for dinner.

IA3, IIE1

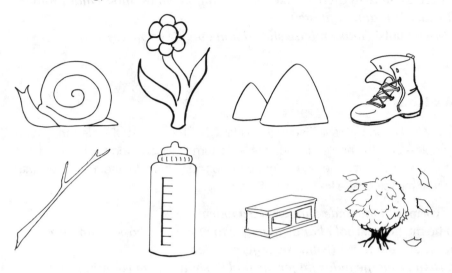

32 Skunk Rhyme

Teach the American Sign Language sign SKUNK and use it as you act out this rhyme.

I am a skunk. *(sign SKUNK)*
My fur is all black,
Except for the white stripe
That runs down my back. *(sign SKUNK slowly, emphasizing stripe)*
Don't make me mad.
If you do, I think
I'll spray you like this—psssssssss
And then you will stink! *(hold nose)*

IC2

Sea Animals

33 Down, Down Deep in the Ocean Blue

At the beginning of each verse, wrap one hand around the other fist to make the rock. When you reveal the animal at the end of each verse, lift the top hand and do the sign with the bottom hand, so it appears as if the animal is coming out from under the rock.

Down, down deep in the ocean blue
Under this rock hides a surprise for you!
It's got gills, and a tail that goes swish.
Can you guess? It is a . . . fish!

Down, down deep in the ocean blue
Under this rock hides a surprise for you!
It's small and pink, it's quite an imp.
Can you guess? It is a . . . shrimp!

Down, down deep in the ocean blue
Under this rock hides a surprise for you!
It's got claws that love to grab.
Can you guess? It is a . . . crab!

IC2

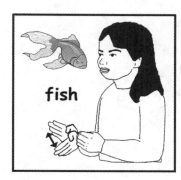

34 5 Little Fish Flannelboard

1 little fish gliding through the ocean blue.
Another dashed out of a sunken ship, and then there were 2.
2 little fish swimming through a coral tree,
Out pops another, and then there were 3.
3 little fish dove to the ocean floor,
They found another, and then there were 4.
4 little fish practicing their dives,
Another joined them, and then there were 5.

IC2, IIA1, IIB1

35 *I'm the Biggest Thing in the Ocean* **Flannelboard**

Based on the book by Kevin Sherry (New York: Dial, 2007)

A giant squid boasts about being the biggest thing in the ocean . . . until something bigger comes along, but his cheery attitude never falters. Reinforce the size concepts in the story by having the children line up the flannelboard animals from largest to smallest.

IA3, IID2

36 Jellyfish

Jellyfish, jellyfish,
You wiggle and you dance. *(wiggle)*
All across the ocean,
Your tentacles do prance. *(move arms like tentacles)*

Jellyfish, jellyfish,
I try to follow you.
But know if I get too close,
What your tentacles can do!
Ouch! *(jump)*

IC2, IE5

Zoo Animals

37 *Monkey See

Act out the words as you say the rhyme.

Hey look at me,
I'm swinging in a tree.
Just you and me,
Feeling fancy free.

Mom and me,
Singing in the tree,
Very loudly,
Ooo, ooo, eee, eee.

Yes we're monkeys
We swing in trees,
And sing woo-wee,
Up in the trees!

IC2

38 *The Swamp Where Gator Hides* Flannelboard

Based on the book by Marianne Berkes (Nevada City, CA: Dawn Publications, 2014)

Who lives in the swamp looking for lunch? An alligator! The cumulative rhyming text of this story brings the Florida Everglades to life. Tell this story using the flannelboard, or follow up a reading of the book by inviting the children to help you retell the story with the flannelboard.

IA1, IA3

39 *Two Little Monkeys Puppet Story

Based on the book by Mem Fox (New York: Simon and Schuster, 2012)

Two little monkeys named Cheeky and Chee have an adventure hiding from a leopard in this simple story that uses the rhythms of the familiar nursery rhyme "Two Little Birds." Tell the story using two monkey puppets and pretend the children are leopards.

IA1, IA3

40 *A Zoo on Our Heads

Use the tune of "Pig on Her Head" by Laurie Berkner—found on *Buzz Buzz* (New York: Two Tomatoes, 1998)—to share a silly song with the children. Pass out animal puppets or die-cut shapes of animals, and invite the children to place them on their heads as you sing the song. This song can be used for farm, zoo, jungle, or pet storytimes—simply adapt the animals you use to your theme. Here are three different ways to use this song in storytime:

1. Give each child a different puppet. Then go around and sing a verse using each child's name. This works especially well for small groups or as an activity to help the children learn and remember one another's names.

   Katie has a sheep on her head,

   Katie has a sheep on her head,

   Katie has a sheep on her head,

   She keeps it there all day.

2. Pass out the same animal to each child. Then sing the following song. (The pace and simple actions of this version make it ideal for babies and toddlers, though preschoolers will also enjoy the silliness!)

   Put your monkey on your head,

   Put your monkey on your head,

   Put your monkey on your head,

   Now jump up and down.

   Put your monkey on your knee . . . now turn 'round and 'round.

   Put your monkey on your ear . . . now stomp stomp stomp your feet.

Put your monkey on your foot . . . now swing your arms like this.

Put your monkey on your hand . . . now sit yourself back down.

3. For older preschoolers and elementary age children, turn this song into an attention and response activity by passing out different animals to each child. The children must listen for their animal and do the associated actions.

If you have a chicken on your head,

If you have a chicken on your head,

If you have a chicken on your head,

Then jump jump up and down.

Other suggested actions:

▶ . . . turn yourself around.

▶ . . . clap clap clap three times.

▶ . . . flap flap flap your wings.

▶ . . . stomp your feet like this.

▶ . . . wiggle wiggle wiggle your hips.

▶ . . . stand up on tiptoes.

▶ . . . wave your arms like this.

▶ . . . toss it in the air.

▶ . . . dance around like this.

IE5

More Entries Related to This Topic

Recommended Books

Nat the Cat Can Sleep Like That by Victoria Allen. Ontario, Canada: Pajama Press, 2013.

Panda and Polar Bear by Matthew J. Baek. New York: Dial, 2009.

Row, Row, Row Your Boat by Jane Cabrera. New York: Holiday House, 2014.

Meow Said the Cow by Emma Dodd. New York: Scholastic, 2009.

I Am Cow, Hear Me Moo by Jill Esbaum. New York: Dial Books for Young Readers, 2014.

Pond Babies by Cathryn Falwell. Camden, ME: Down East Books, 2011.

The Farmer's Away! Baa! Neigh! by Anne Vittur Kennedy. Somerville, MA: Candlewick, 2014.

*Say Hello Like This by Mary Murphy. Somerville, MA: Candlewick, 2014.

The Nest Where I Like to Rest: Sign Language for Animals by Dawn Babb Prochovnic. Edina, MN: Magic Wagon, 2012.

Buddy and the Bunnies in Don't Play with Your Food by Bob Shea. New York: Hyperion, 2014.

4

Around the World

FOR LOTS MORE storytime fun from around the world, be sure to check out our book *Multicultural Storytime Magic* (ALA Editions, 2012).

Africa

41 Clever Jackal: An African Folktale Flannelboard (adapted traditional)

One day long ago, Jackal was nosing among the rocks. He thought he might find a rat
or a lizard for his lunch. He was so busy sniffing around that he didn't notice until the last minute that Lion was up ahead of him.

"Oh no!" he thought. "I have played so many tricks on Lion that he will be very angry
when he sees me and might use his sharp teeth and fierce claws on me! What
will I do?"

But Jackal wasn't known as Clever Jackal for nothing.

"Help! Help!" he cried. He cowered down, looking at the rocks above.

Of course Lion heard him, and he turned around in surprise. "What's the matter,
Jackal?" he asked.

"Oh, help! Help!" Jackal howled. "Oh, great Lion! There is no time to lose! Those
great rocks above us are about to fall and crush us! Oh, Lion, save us! Use your
mighty strength to hold up the rocks!"

Lion swelled with pride. "I am very strong," he said, and put his shoulder under the rock.

"Oh, thank you, mighty Lion!" said Jackal. "I will fetch that log over there to prop under the rock, and we will both be saved!"

Do you think Jackal fetched the log?

He didn't! He ran away as fast as he could.

Who knows how long Lion stayed under the rock before he realized that it wasn't going to fall and that Jackal had tricked him? But we do know that Jackal is still out there playing tricks to this day!

IA1, IA3

42 Frogs, Frogs, Where Are You Going? A Rhyme from the Democratic Republic of Congo (adapted traditional)

Frogs, frogs, where are you going? *(hop like a frog)*
We are going to market, to market.
If they catch you, what will they do?
They will turn us all into lizards. *(flick tongue like a lizard)*

Lizards, lizards, where are you going?
We are going to market, to market.
If they catch you, what will they do?
They will turn us all into elephants! *(move arm like a trunk and stomp like an elephant)*

Continue, allowing each child to suggest an animal and changing the movements to match.

IE5, IE6

43 Walking through the Bush: A Zulu Chant Flannelboard (adapted traditional)

Walking through the bush, what do I see?
I can see a snake looking at me.
Walking through the bush, what do I see?
I can see a tortoise looking at me.
Walking through the bush, what do I see?
I can see an elephant looking at me.
Walking through the bush, what do I see?
I can see an eagle looking at me.

Walking through the bush, what do I see?
I can see *you* looking at me!

IC2

Asia

44 **Chopsticks**

Give each child a pair of chopsticks to grab the pretend foods, or have the children use their fingers as pretend chopsticks.

So many foods, what shall we eat?
We'll use our chopsticks to grab our treats!
Wontons, wontons, get them while they're hot,
Use your chopsticks to grab them from the pot.
Spring rolls, spring rolls are such a delight,
Chopsticks aren't needed, hold them in your hands tight!
Lo mein, lo mein, its long noodles wiggle,
Using chopsticks to eat them will make you giggle!
Dumplings, dumplings so soft and steamy,
My brother grabs mine, what a meanie!
Kung Po, Kung Po, hold on tight,
Eating pieces from our chopsticks finishes the night.

IC2

45 **Let Me Pass: A Japanese Game** (traditional)

This game is similar to "London Bridge Is Falling Down." Two children face each other and lift their joined hands to make an arch, and the other children walk through the arch in a line. The child who is under the arch at the end of the rhyme is "caught." The words of the song refer to the traditional offering made to the sky god on a child's seventh birthday.

Let me pass, let me pass.
What is this narrow pathway here?
It's the narrow pathway of the sky god's shrine.
Please allow me to pass through.
Those without good reason shall not pass.
To celebrate this child's seventh birthday,
I've come to dedicate my offering.

Going in will be fine, fine, but returning will be scary.
It's scary but
Let me pass, let me pass.

IE1

46 ***One Two Three: A Chinese Counting Rhyme** (adapted traditional)

1, 2, 3
Climb up the mountain. *(make fingers of one hand climb up the palm of the other)*
4, 5, 6
Somersault! *(make fingers tumble down from top of palm)*
7, 8, 9
Bounce the ball! *(mime bouncing a ball)*
Put out 2 hands *(hold hands out in front of you)*
10 fingers in all! *(wiggle fingers)*

IIA1

Australia

47 ***5 Little Koalas Flannelboard** (to the tune of "10 Green Bottles")

1 little koala playing in the sun.
1 little koala playing in the sun.
And if 1 more koala should come and join the fun,
There'll be 2 little koalas playing in the sun.

2 little koalas . . .
3 little koalas . . .
4 little koalas . . .

5 little koalas playing in the sun.
5 little koalas playing in the sun.
And when no more koalas came to join the fun,
5 little koalas went home when day was done.

IIA1

48 **Johnny and Jane: An Australian Nursery Rhyme** (adapted traditional)

Johnny and Jane and Jack and Lou, *(hold out one hand, then the other, then slap one
    knee, then the other)*
Butler's Stairs through Woolloomooloo, *(mime walking)*
Woolloomooloo, and 'cross the Domain, *(take two steps forward)*
Round the block, and home again! *(walk in a circle back to starting point)*
Heigh, ho! *(raise hands in air)*

Tipsy-toe, *(tiptoe)*
Give us a kiss and away we go! *(blow a kiss and then run in place)*

IC2

---

49 ***Kangaroo Song** (adapted traditional; to the tune of "Here We Go 'Round the Mulberry Bush")

Have the children jump and hop in a circle as you sing this song. Begin slowly and then repeat, increasing speed each time.

Bumpety jumpety hop and go one,
Hop and go one, hop and go one.
Sleep with an eye open out in the sun,
Bumpety jumpety hop.

IC2

---

50 *Over in Australia: Amazing Animals Down Under* **Flannelboard**

Based on the book by Marianne Berkes (Nevada City, CA: Dawn Publications, 2011)

This song story, based on "Over in the Meadow," features Australian animals from crocodiles to emus.

IIA1

Europe

51 **The Ant and the Crumb: A Folktale from Spain Flannelboard**
(adapted traditional)

Once upon a time there was a little red ant who lived in a cornfield. Every day she went out with the other ants and gathered corn. But one day . . . one day she found something that looked different. It smelled sweet and yummy. It wasn't corn—it was cake!

But the other ants were so busy carrying corn back and forth that they didn't even hear her when she called to them to come help her carry it.

"What shall I do?" she said. "For I am too small to carry this piece of cake alone. I know! I will ask El Gallo to help! He is big and strong!"

So she scurried to the nearby farmyard, where El Gallo—the rooster—was strutting around. "El Gallo!" she squeaked. "Please, I need your help! You are big and strong, and surely you can help me move the piece of cake I have found!"

El Gallo strutted and preened his feathers. "I am big and strong," he said, "but I am much too busy to help a tiny thing like you. Be gone!"

But then El Gallo froze—for he had heard a howl nearby. It sounded like this: A-wooooooo! "It is El Coyote!" cried El Gallo in fear. "I must hide!" And he disappeared around the barn in a twinkling.

The little red ant followed the sound of the howling, for she knew it would lead her to El Coyote, and he was even bigger and stronger than El Gallo—maybe he would help her move the piece of cake. She found El Coyote at the top of a rise near the farmyard, howling with glee.

When he stopped to take a breath, the little red ant hurried forward. "El Coyote!" she squeaked. "Please, I need your help! You are big and strong, and surely you can help me move the piece of cake I have found!"

El Coyote puffed up with pride. "I am big and strong," he said, "but I am much too busy to help a tiny thing like you. Be gone!"

But then El Coyote froze—for he had heard whistling coming up the road nearby. It sounded like this: *(whistle a tune)*. "It is El Hombre!" cried El Coyote in fear. "I must hide!" And he disappeared down the other side of the hill in a twinkling.

The little red ant followed the sound of the whistling, for she knew it would lead her to El Hombre—the man—and he was even bigger and stronger than El Coyote. Maybe he would help her move the piece of cake. She found El Hombre walking down the lane.

The little red ant crawled up onto his shoe, and up his leg, up his arm, to his shoulder, and found a place right next to his ear. "El Hombre!" she shouted as loudly as she could. "Please, I need your help! You are big and strong, and surely you can help me move the piece of cake I have found!"

"AAAAARRRRGGGGH! A bug! Something is in my ear! Get it off! Get it off!" cried El Hombre in fright. He brushed the little red ant away, and she tumbled to the ground. Down the lane ran El Hombre in fright.

"Well," thought the little red ant. "I frightened El Hombre, who is so big and strong that he frightened El Coyote. And El Coyote is

so big and strong that he frightened El Gallo. That means that I am bigger and stronger than all of them! Surely something as big and strong as that can handle a little piece of cake all by herself."

And so she did. And it was mighty delicious, too.

IID2

52 A Charming Song: A British Nursery Rhyme Flannelboard (traditional)

"Bow-wow," says the dog;
"Mew, mew," says the cat;
"Grunt, grunt," goes the hog;
And "Squeak!" goes the rat.
"Chirp, chirp," says the sparrow;
"Caw, caw," says the crow;
"Quack, quack," says the duck;
And the cuckoo you know.
So with sparrows and cuckoos,
With rats and with dogs,
With ducks and with crows,
With cats and with hogs!
A fine song I've made
To please you, my dear,
And if it's well sung,
'Twill be charming to hear.

IC2

53 Grandpa Rode His Horse: An Icelandic Nursery Rhyme (adapted traditional)

Have the children trot like horses as you say this rhyme. Repeat the rhyme and have the children take turns calling out other grocery items Grandpa might get in the third line. If desired, make this a writing readiness activity by having the children brainstorm a grocery list before you introduce the rhyme.

Grandpa rode his horse, Red,
South, south of town.
He went to get some sugar and bread,
A little bit of each.

ID2, IE6

54 Ladybug Legends Flannelboard

In many cultures around the world, ladybugs are thought to be lucky. Each line in this rhyme draws from a different cultural tradition about ladybugs.

5 little ladybugs flying through the door,
We'll have so much money, we'll never be poor. *(Folklore)*
4 little ladybugs land on my head,
I'll get a new hat, so they said. *(Britain)*
3 little ladybugs flying all around,
The farmers know that crops will abound! *(Britain)*
2 little ladybugs land in my hand,
I wish to be married, let's book the band. *(Sweden)*
1 little ladybug, I feel sick today,
Please land on me so my illness goes away! *(France)*

      IIA1

55 *A Little Story about a Big Turnip: A Russian Folktale* Flannelboard

Based on the book by Tatiana Zunshine (Columbus, OH: Pumpkin House, 2003)

When a turnip is too big for the farmer to harvest alone, he calls on everyone in his family, even the pets, to help.

      IA1, IA3, IID2

North America

56 The Cazuela That the Farm Maiden Stirred *Flannelboard*

Based on the book by Samantha R. Vamos (Watertown, MA: Charlesbridge, 2011)

In this cumulative tale that follows the pattern of "The House That Jack Built," a Mexican farm maiden makes *arroz con leche* (rice pudding).

      IA1, IA3

57 Moose Rhyme

In the northern Canadian lands,
Where the wind does blow, *(move hands side to side to imitate wind)*
You might find a giant creature
Walking through the snow. *(walk in place)*

It's not a polar bear or hare, *(hulk like a bear, twitch nose like a hare)*
It's not a Canada Goose. *(flap arms like wings)*
With shaggy brown fur and antlers like this, *(hold hands to temples like antlers)*
You're looking at a . . . moose!

IC2

South America

58 A la rueda, rueda / 'Round, 'Round the Ring: A Circle Rhyme from Venezuela (traditional)

Introduce this circle rhyme and then ask the children if they know any others like it. Discuss its similarity to "Ring Around the Rosie" and how children in many cultures play similar games.

A la rueda, rueda (ah la roo-AY-da, roo-AY-da)
de pan y canela (dee PAN ee kan-AY-la)
dame un besito (DAH-may oon BAY-see-toe)
y vete a la escuela (ee VET-ay ah la es-koo-AY-la)
y si no quieres ir, (ee see no kee-AIR-es eer)
vete a dormir. (VET-ay ah dor-MEER)

'Round, 'round the ring *(hold hands and move in a circle for the first two lines)*
Of bread and cinnamon.
Give me a kiss *(everyone moves into the center with hands still joined)*
And off you go to school. *(move circle back out)*
And if you don't want to go, *(move in a circle)*
Then go, go to sleep! *(all fall down)*

     IE5

59 La lechuza / The Barn Owl: A Song from Argentina (to the tune of "Frère Jacques")

As you sing the song in English or Spanish, invite the children to flap their wings silently like the barn owl. Move in a silent circle around your storytime area.

La lechuza, la lechuza (la LAY-kyu-za, la LAY-kyu-za)
hace ¡Shhhh! hace ¡Shhhh! (AH-say shhhh, AH-say shhhh)
Hágamos silencio, (ah-GAH-mos see-len-see-oh)
como la lechuza (koh-mo la LAY-kyu-za)
que hace ¡Shhhh! que hace ¡Shhhh! (kay AH-say shhhh)

The barn owl, the barn owl
Says *shhhh!* Says *shhhh!*
Let's be very quiet, quiet as the barn owl,
Who says *shhhh!* Who says *shhhh!*

     IE5

More Entries Related to This Topic

Recommended Books

Ten Little Fingers and Ten Little Toes by Mem Fox. Orlando, FL: Harcourt, 2008.

By Day, By Night by Amy Gibson. Honesdale, PA: Boyds Mills Press, 2014.

It's a Small World: I Love School! by Calliope Glass. New York: Disney, 2012.

Peek! A Thai Hide-and-Seek by Minfong Ho. Cambridge, MA: Candlewick, 2004.

Auntie Yang's Great Soybean Picnic by Ginnie Lo. New York: Lee and Low, 2012.

Take Me Out to the Yakyu by Aaron Meshon. New York: Atheneum, 2013.

Bee-bim Bop! by Linda Sue Park. New York: Clarion, 2005.

Welcome, Brown Bird by Mary Lyn Ray. Orlando, FL: Harcourt, 2004.

What Can You Do with a Rebozo? / ¿Qué Puedes hacer con un rebozo? by Carmen Tafolla. Berkeley, CA: Tricycle, 2008.

Green Is a Chile Pepper: A Book of Colors by Roseanne Greenfield Thong. San Francisco, CA: Chronicle, 2014.

5

At Home

Around the House

60 Cleaning Time (to the tune of "I'm Gonna Wash That Man Right Outta My Hair")

I'm gonna wash that dirt right off of my floor.
I'm gonna wash that dirt right off of my floor.
I'm gonna wash that dirt right off of my floor.
And let it shine like new.

I'm gonna wave that dust right off of my things . . .
And let them shine like new.

Don't try to ignore it,
Clean up, clean up,
Wash the floors, dust the desk,
Vacuum carpet, wipe the counters,
And then it's time to play!
Yay!

IC2, IE5

61 Cleaning Song (to the tune of "Three Blind Mice")

Use the sign CLEAN with this song.

Clean, clean, clean,
I like to clean.
Clean, clean, clean,
I like to clean.
I wipe down the windows and tidy my toys,
I use the big vacuum that makes lot of noise.
Let's clean up the house now, you good girls and boys.
It's clean, clean, clean.

IC2, IE5

62 Home Flannelboard

H is for house, that's where we begin.
O is for open the door and come in!
M is for mother and father and family.
E is for everyone who comes to visit me!
Put them together, they spell out a place
That always brings a smile to my face.
H-O-M-E! Home!

IC2, IC3

63 House Cleaning (to the tune of "Hush Little Baby")

Place the house on the board. As you introduce each object, invite the children to help you figure out where it belongs.

We're cleaning up the house today,
We're going to put all the things away.
I've got a cup. Where does it go?
If you know, then tell us so.

Children may have a variety of answers for the objects. Take time to discuss that cleaning may be done differently in each home. Repeat with other objects.

IC2, IE5

64 I Am a House

I am a house with 4 strong walls,
1, 2, 3, 4,
I count them all. *(turn in a circle, placing hands out flat in front of you as if touching each wall)*
I have a door to let you come and go, *(mime opening a door in front of you)*
And to make light, I've a big window. *(lean to the side and draw a large window shape in the front "wall" with your index fingers)*
A nice flat floor below have I, *(stoop and run hands flat over the ground)*
And the roof above keeps you warm and dry. *(move hands above you in a peak to show the roof)*

IC2, IIA1, IIA4

65 Mama's Chores

Act out the words of the rhyme.

Mama hangs the towels one by one,
On the line in the warmth of the sun.
With a swish, swish, swish of her broom,
Mama sweeps the dust from the room.
Mama scrubs the dishes and wipes them dry,
With a bubble and a squeak, and a my-oh-my!
With a vroom, vroom, vroom and a smooth slide,
Mama vacuums the rooms with a glide.
At the end of the day in the moonlight,
Mama puts her feet up and says goodnight.

IC2, IE5

66 Moving Song (to the tune of "The Farmer in the Dell")

Explain that you have an imaginary moving truck and you need the children to help you pack up the house to move to a new place. Then sing the song.

We're packing up the house,
We're packing up the house.
We're packing up, it's time to move,
We're packing up the house.

Now we're packing up the kitchen! What kinds of things will we find in the kitchen?

Take answers from the children, then mime moving kitchen objects as you sing the next verse.

We're packing up the kitchen,
We're packing up the kitchen.
We're packing up, it's time to move,
We're packing up the kitchen.

Repeat with living room, bathroom, bedroom, playroom, and den. If desired, make this a writing readiness activity by writing the children's answers on a flipchart, chalkboard, or whiteboard and reading the answers out loud together.

IC2, ID7, IE5, IE6

67 What Do I See at Home? Flannelboard

Place the items on the flannelboard. For younger children, you may wish to limit the selection to four items at a time.

I see something in my house that is round and fun to play with. What is it? It's my ball!
I see something in my house that I can sit on. What is it? It's my chair!
I see something in my house that is so soft and says "purrrrr." What is it? It's my cat!
I see something in my house that lights up the night. What is it? It's a lamp!
I see something in my house that is yummy to eat with butter or honey. What is it? It's a piece of bread!
I see something in my house that keeps my head warm. What is it? It's my hat!
I see something in my house that tastes so sweet and crunches when I bite into it. What is it? It's an apple!
I see something in my house that helps me rest at night. What is it? It's my bed!

IE1, IE3, IE5

More Entries Related to This Topic

Mailbox Rhyme, p. 127

Telephone Rhyme, p. 136

Washing My Car, p. 165

Bath Time

68 ***Bath Time Hokey Pokey** (to the tune of "The Hokey Pokey")

You wash your right arm up,
You wash your right arm down,
You wash your right arm up,
And you wash it all about.
You dip it in the water and you splash it all around.
That's what it's all about.

You wash your left arm up . . .
You wash your right leg up . . .
You wash your left leg up . . .
You wash your tummy up . . .
You wash your hair up . . .
You wash your whole self up . . .

IC2, IE5

69 ***Bubble on My Nose** (to the tune of "If You're Happy and You Know It")

There's a bubble on my nose, on my nose,
A bath time bubble on my nose, on my nose.
Oh, how you suppose that bubble got on my nose?
There's a bubble on my nose, on my nose.

. . . on my knee . . . I'm clean as can be, with a bubble on my knee . . .
. . . on my hair . . . you don't have to stare at the bubble on my hair . . .
. . . on my arm . . . it's not doing any harm, that bubble on my arm . . .
. . . on my tummy . . . oh, isn't it funny, that bubble on my tummy . . .
. . . on my ear . . . no need to fear that bubble on my ear . . .

IC2, IE5

More Entries Related to This Topic

Oh No, Little Dragon! Flannelboard, p. 77
Rubber Ducky, p. 135

Bedtime

70 *Baby Love

Hugs in the morning and hugs at night,
I like when Mama squeezes me tight. *(wrap arms around yourself)*
Kisses in the morning and kisses at night,
Daddy makes smooching noises whenever I'm in sight. *(make smooching noise)*
Cuddles in the morning and cuddles at night,
A blanket, a book, and it's time to say goodnight. *(wave goodnight)*

IC2, IE5

71 *Bedtime (to the tune of "Here We Go 'Round the Mulberry Bush")

Act out the words as you sing the song.

This is the way I wash my face, wash my face, wash my face,
This is the way I wash my face before I go to bed.

This is the way I brush my teeth . . . before I go to bed.
This is the way I put on my PJs . . . before I go to bed.
This is the way I climb into bed . . . when the day is done.
This is the way I say goodnight . . . with a big kiss! Smooch!

IC2, IE5

72 *5 Little Stars

Place the stars on the board. Remove them as each star says "goodnight."

5 little stars twinkle in the sky,
They're so sleepy and so am I.
5 little stars shine their light,
1 reads a bedtime story and says "goodnight."
4 little stars shine their light,
1 gets a last drink of water and says "goodnight."
3 little stars shine their light,
1 fluffs his pillow and says "goodnight."
2 little stars shine their light,
1 has a *yawn* and says "goodnight."
1 little star shines his light,
He blows you a kiss and says "goodnight."

IC2, IIA1, IIA4, IIB1

73 ***Llama Mama, Llama Baby***

Use this fingerplay as a follow-up to *Llama Llama Red Pajama* by Anna Dewdney (New York: Viking, 2005) or your favorite llama story.

Join your middle and ring fingers and your thumb, with your index and pinky fingers sticking up, to make the llamas' heads.

Llama Mama, Llama Baby *(make llamas with both hands; hold the baby llama
    slightly lower than the mama)*
"Time for bed! *(move Llama Mama hand as if speaking)*
Come along, Llama Baby,
Lay down your head."

Llama Baby runs away: *(make Llama Baby run away)*
"No, no, no!"
Llama Mama follows after *(make Llama Mama follow)*
Just like so.

Llama Mama tickles, *(tickle Llama Baby with Llama Mama)*
Llama Mama hugs, *(hug Llama Baby with Llama Mama)*
Llama Baby giggles, *(move Llama Baby as if giggling)*
And cuddles in snug. *(snuggle two llamas together)*

Llama Mama, Llama Baby *(say this verse quietly this time)*
"Time for bed! *(move Llama Mama as if speaking)*
Come along, Llama Baby,
Lay down your head." *(lay Llama Baby sideways as if on a pillow)*

"Settle down, Llama Baby,
Just like this.
Give your Llama Mama
A goodnight kiss." *(make two llamas kiss)*

      IC2, IE5

74 ***Mama Bear's Babies Flannelboard Story***

Cut out many bears in different colors, enough for each child.

Once upon a time, there was a Mama Bear who had many, many babies. Her baby
    bears had fur in many different colors! They loved to play all day in the woods.
    (pass out one bear to each child)
The baby bears played and played. They sang some of their favorite songs. What are
    some of your favorite songs? *(sing a few favorite songs suggested by the group)*
They jumped, and ran in place, and danced. *(encourage children to do these actions
    with you)* How else do you think they played? *(take suggestions from the
    children)*
Well, soon it was time to come home and have dinner and get ready for bed! Mama
    Bear went to the mouth of the cave and called, "Red bears! Red bears! Time to
    come home!" And all of the red bears ran home for dinner. *(encourage children*

with red bears to place them on the flannelboard; repeat with other colors until all the bears are home)

Then she sat them around the dinner table and counted them to make sure they were all home. *(count the bears)*

They were all home! They ate up their dinners, and then got ready for bed. How many kisses did Mama Bear give them before they went to sleep? One for each bear! Will you blow a kiss to each bear? Let's count our kisses! *(blow a kiss to each bear; if desired, end by singing the bears a lullaby)*

IE5, IIA1, IIA4, IIA5, IID3

More Entries Related to This Topic

*5 Tired Knights Flannelboard, p. 75

Good Night, Knight Flannelboard, p. 75

*Mommy, Mommy, p. 82

*Night and Day Flannelboard Game, p. 110

**Night Owl* Flannelboard and Sound Story, p. 13

Our House, p. 82

**Small Bunny's Blue Blanket* Scarf Story, p. 135

T-E-E-T-H Flannelboard/Magnetboard, p. 10

Under the Nighttime Sky, p. 111

Wow! Said the Owl Flannelboard, p. 111

Recommended Books

Daisy Gets Dressed by Clare Beaton. Cambridge, MA: Barefoot Books, 2005.

**Here We Go Round the Mulberry Bush* by Jane Cabrera. New York: Holiday House, 2010.

**Small Blue and the Deep Dark Night* by Jon Davis. New York: Houghton Mifflin, 2014.

**Sleepyheads* by Sandra J. Howatt. New York: Beach Lane Books, 2014.

On My Way to the Bath by Sarah Maizes. New York: Walker, 2012.

Sleep Like a Tiger by Mary Logue. New York: Houghton Mifflin, 2012.

Kitty Cat, Kitty Cat, Are You Going to Sleep? by Bill Martin Jr. Tarrytown, NY: Marshall Cavendish, 2011.

Kitty Cat, Kitty Cat, Are You Waking Up? by Bill Martin Jr. Tarrytown, NY: Marshall Cavendish, 2008.

Little Oink by Amy Krouse Rosenthal. San Francisco: Chronicle, 2009.

Time for Bed, Baby Ted by Debra Sartell. New York: Holiday House, 2010.

Dinosaur vs. Bedtime by Bob Shea. New York: Hyperion, 2008.

6
Bugs and Insects

Ants

75 Ant Parade Flannelboard Rhyme

1 little ant marched in a line,
Off to a picnic where he could dine.
He came back and told a friend,
And they started out again.

2 little ants marched in a line . . .
3 little ants marched in a line . . .
4 little ants marched in a line . . .

5 little ants marched in a line,
Off to a picnic where they could dine.
They came back with their bellies full,
And decided to lounge by the pool!

IC2, IIA1, IIA4, IIA5

76 The Little Ant

There was a little ant *(crouch down like an ant)*
And everybody said, "You can't
Lift that big bread crumb—
You're too small!"

But she grunted and groaned *(mime lifting something heavy)*
And she carried it home *(raise imaginary item over head)*
And I guess she showed
Them all!

> **IC2**

77 This Little Ant: A Rhyme from Mexico (traditional)

This little ant worked with might and main. *(wiggle finger across opposite palm)*
Bringing in wood till it started to rain.
Then to her anthill off she hurried, *(turn palm over and cup it)*
Into her little house she scurried. *(move index finger into cupped palm)*

> **IC2**

Bees

78 *Buzzy Bumblebee (to the tune of "Sticky Bubblegum")

Use pom-poms or the following Bumblebee Stick Puppet Craft as you sing this song. Make the bee buzz around in the air until it lands on the last line.

Buzzy buzzy buzzy bumblebee
Bumblebee, bumblebee.
Buzzy buzzy buzzy bumblebee
Landing on my nose.

Repeat using different body parts.

> **IC2, IE5**

79 *Bumblebee Stick Puppet Craft

Materials needed: bumblebee shape (from template), crayons, craft stick, glue, other decorating materials as desired

1. Cut out the bumblebee shape.

2. Color the bumblebee.

3. Decorate the bumblebee as desired. For example, you may wish to attach pipe cleaners for antennae.

4. Glue the bumblebee to a craft stick.

5. Make your bumblebee fly through the air! Use it for the preceding "Buzzy Bumblebee" song.

Caterpillars and Butterflies

80 **Butterfly Dance**

Butterflies flutter from flower to flower, *(flap arms like wings)*
Sipping sweet nectar hour after hour.
Butterflies spread their wings and fly
All day long high in the sky.
But when it's time to say goodnight,
Butterflies sleep with wings furled tight. *(pull arms close to body)*

       IC2, IE5

81 **Caterpillar Song** (to the tune of "Lollipop")

Caterpillar, caterpillar, fuzzy, wuzzy caterpillar. *(sign CATERPILLAR during this chorus)*
Caterpillar, caterpillar, fuzzy, wuzzy caterpillar.
Caterpillar!

First we see a caterpillar on a leaf. *(wiggle index finger on opposite palm to show caterpillar on leaf)*
He's gonna eat all he can eat. *(mime eating)*
Then he starts to spin a cocoon like this, *(roll hands to represent spinning)*
And he becomes a chrysalis. *(cup palms together to represent chrysalis)*

Now he's a chrysalis, chrysalis, now he's a chrysalis.
Chrysalis, chrysalis, now he's a chrysalis.
Chrysalis!

What's going on inside the chrysalis?
There's gonna be a metamorphosis.
When it opens up, we'll have a big
    surprise, *(open palms)*
'Cause now we see a butterfly! *(sign BUTTERFLY)*
Now he's a butterfly, butterfly,
    beautiful butterfly.
Butterfly, butterfly, beautiful butterfly.
Butterfly!

      IC2, IE4, IE5, IE6

82 Little Caterpillar

Little caterpillar, I know a secret about you,
You munch and munch and munch, *(mime eating)*
So many leaves to eat through!

Little caterpillar, I know a secret about you,
You spin yourself in a tight cocoon, *(spin in a circle)*
So many days to sleep through!

Little caterpillar, I know a secret about you,
You bust through the cocoon, *(spread arms and flap like wings)*
And show off your wings that are new!

        IC2, IE5

Spiders

83 Spinning Spider Song (to the tune of "Row, Row, Row Your Boat")

Spin, spin, spin your web,
Lace patterns in the dew.
Patiently sit and wait for hours,
Till dinner gets stuck in the goo!

        IC2, IE5

84 *Spider Song (to the tune of "The Farmer in the Dell")

Teach the sign SPIDER and then make the sign travel over the body parts indicated in the song.

There's a spider on my foot,
There's a spider on my foot.
It's crawling up my leg
And it's resting on my knee.

There's a spider on my knee,
There's a spider on my knee.
It's crawling up my thigh
And it's resting on my hip.

There's a spider on my hip,
There's a spider on my hip.
It's crawling up my tummy
And it's resting on my shoulder.

spider

There's a spider on my shoulder,
There's a spider on my shoulder.

It's crawling up my face
And it's resting on my head.

There's a spider on my head,
There's a spider on my head.
It's jumping to the floor
And it's running far away!
Bye spider!

IC2, IE5

Other Bugs and Insects

85 Cicadas Flannelboard

1 cicada, 2 cicadas, 3 cicadas, 4.
5 cicadas, 6 cicadas, flying 'round my door.
7 cicadas, 8 cicadas, 9 cicadas, 10.
It'll be years before we see them again!

Fun fact: When cicada eggs hatch, the cicadas, called nymphs, drop to
the ground, where they burrow down and stay for years. Some types of
cicadas stay underground for seventeen years before they come out again!

IC2, IIA1

86 Dragonfly, Dragonfly

Dragonfly, dragonfly, flutter around. *(mime flapping wings)*
Dragonfly, dragonfly, land on the ground. *(crouch down low)*
Dragonfly, dragonfly, fly up high. *(stand on tiptoe)*
Dragonfly, dragonfly, touch the sky. *(reach arms up high)*
Dragonfly, dragonfly, fly down low. *(crouch and flap arms)*
Dragonfly, dragonfly, land on my toe. *(point to toe)*
Dragonfly, dragonfly, there is fading light, *(move hands in front of face)*
Dragonfly, dragonfly, time to say goodnight. *(wave)*

IC2

87 Firefly (to the tune of "Twinkle, Twinkle Little Star")

Twinkle, twinkle firefly,
Flashing in the nighttime sky.
With your tempting patterned light,
Everyone squeals with delight.
Twinkle, twinkle firefly,
Flashing in the nighttime sky.

IC2, IE5

88 ***5 Green Grasshoppers Flannelboard**

5 green grasshoppers jumping up and down,
1 leapt so high the wind carried him into town.
4 green grasshoppers jumping high in the air,
1 leapt so far she landed at the county fair.
3 green grasshoppers jumping all around,
1 leapt so much he got dizzy and hit the ground.
2 green grasshoppers jumping from tree to tree,
1 leapt away and said, "You can't catch me!"
1 green grasshopper jumping all alone,
She decided it was time to jump on home!

IC2, IE5, IIA1, IIA4, IIB1

89 ***Ladybug, Ladybug**

Ladybug, ladybug, give a hop. *(hop)*
Ladybug, ladybug, show your spots. *(turn and spread arms like wings)*
Ladybug, ladybug, fly around. *(flap arms)*
Ladybug, ladybug, land on the ground. *(sit down)*

IC2, IE5

More Entries Related to This Topic

The Ant and the Crumb: A Folktale from Spain Flannelboard, p. 37

Butterfly Beanbag Rhyme, p. 116

Garden Friends, p. 80

Ladybug Legends Flannelboard, p. 40

*Spider Crawl, p. 9

Recommended Books

The Monkey and the Bee by C. P. Bloom. New York: Abrams, 2015.

Some Bugs by Angela DiTerlizzi. New York: Beach Lane Books, 2014.

Fly! by Karl Edwards. New York: Knopf, 2015.

Beetle Bop by Denise Fleming. New York: Harcourt, 2007.

Pig and Small by Alex Latimer. Atlanta: Peachtree, 2014.

Bug on a Bike by Chris Monroe. Minneapolis, MN: Carolrhoda Books, 2014.

Buggy Bug by Chris Raschka. New York: Abrams Appleseed, 2014.

Swamp Chomp by Lola Schaefer. New York: Holiday House, 2014.

Bugs Galore by Peter Stein. Somerville, MA: Candlewick, 2012.

The Big Blue Thing on the Hill by Yuval Zommer. Somerville, MA:
    Templar Books, 2015.

7
Concepts

· ·

Alphabet

90 Betty Botter (adapted traditional)

Invite the children to listen carefully to this rhyme and jump up each time they hear a *B* sound.

Betty Botter bought some butter.
"But," she said, "this butter's bitter.
If I put it in my batter,
It will make my batter bitter.
But a bit of better butter
Will make my batter better!"
So, Betty Botter bought
A bit of butter
Better than her bitter butter
And the batter was not bitter!

      IC2, IE5

91 **Rhythm Stick ABCs**

Give each child a pair of rhythm sticks to use as you say this rhyme. Begin by saying the alphabet together, tapping the sticks together once for each letter.

A, A, let's draw an A. *(take one stick and draw a large letter A in the air)*
Point to something that starts with A. *(use stick to point to something in the room that starts with A)*

Take a moment to discuss the A words the children found, then select another letter and repeat the activity.

IC1, IC2

92 **26 Great Letters** (to the tune of "Ten Little Indians")

Use magnetic or felt letters with this song. After each line in the spelling verses, give the children a chance to find the letters, then together sound out the word they spell. Repeat with as many three-letter words as you like.

There are 26 great letters
There are 26 great letters
There are 26 great letters
In our alphabet.

Can you find the letter *C*?
Can you find the letter *A*?
Can you find the letter *T*?
Now put them together.

Repeat with other three-letter words.

IC1, IC2, IC3

Another Entry Related to This Topic

*Pumpkin Patch Match, p. 121

Colors

93 **Colors** (to the tune of "Row, Row, Row Your Boat")

Red, red, red is the color,
The color that I spy.
If you're wearing any red,
Raise your hand up high!

Repeat with other colors.

IC2, IE5, IE6

94 *5 Little Birdies Flannelboard

5 little birdies chirping on my lawn.
The red bird chirped, and then it was gone.
4 little birdies chirping on my lawn.
The blue bird chirped, and then it was gone.
3 little birdies chirping on my lawn.
The yellow bird chirped, and then it was gone.
2 little birdies chirping on my lawn.
The white bird chirped, and then it was gone.
1 little birdy chirping on my lawn.
The black bird chirped, and then it was gone.

IC2, IIA1, IIA4

95 My Favorite Color

Yellow is my favorite color,
It's as bright as the sun,
And when the sun is shining,
The day is super fun!

Red is my favorite color,
It's full of love like my heart,
Flowers grow bright red,
And my dad makes cherry tarts!

Blue is my favorite color,
It's a clear morning and the sky,
The color of my cozy blanket,
And my mom's beautiful eyes.

Green is my favorite color,
A sign of warmer days and spring,
New leaves on the trees,
And my play set with a swing!

IC2, IE5

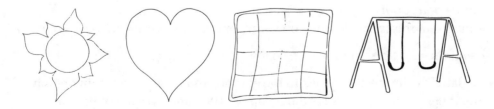

More Entries Related to This Topic

Numbers

96 Carrot Patch Flannelboard/Prop Story

Materials needed: a large rectangle of brown felt, tacky glue, orange popsicle sticks, green felt, sharp scissors

Hold the felt so that the longest sides are at the top and bottom. Make five half-inch horizontal cuts in a row about one-third of the way down. Then fold the felt in half so that the two longer sides come together and glue the seams all the way around. This will be the background of your carrot patch. Place the background on the flannelboard so that the folded side of the felt is at the bottom and the slits are facing out.

To make the carrots, use the template to cut out leaves from green felt and glue them to the tops of the orange popsicle sticks. Then place the carrots in the slits in the felt to show the carrots growing in the ground.

This story requires twenty-five carrots. See the variations following the story for tips on adapting to different groups.

Use a rabbit stuffed animal or puppet to help you tell the story. Begin the story with one carrot in each hole.

Once upon a time there was a bunny who *loved* to count. And his favorite thing to count was *carrots!* One day he went to the garden and what do you think he saw growing there? Carrots! He did a happy little dance. *(make bunny dance and invite children to dance, too)*

Then he said, "I am going to count the carrots! How many carrots do you see in each hole? Yes, I see *one* carrot in each hole. Let's count them together! 1, 2, 3, 4, 5! Oh! Let's count again, but let's add a clap for each hole!" *(clap once for each number as you count)*

"Now, it's time to eat the carrots! Yum yum yum!" *(make rabbit pretend to eat carrots)*

Place two carrots in each hole, fanning them so the tops can be seen.

Well, a while later the bunny went back to the garden, and what do you think he saw growing there? *More* carrots! He did a happy little dance. *(make bunny dance and invite children to dance, too)*

Then he said, "I am going to count the carrots! How many carrots do you see in each hole? Yes, I see *two* carrots in each hole. Let's count them together! 1, 2, 3, 4, 5, 6, 7, 8, 9, 10! Oh! Let's count again, but let's do a new pattern this time. We will slap our knees, and then clap! Like this: slap-*clap*-slap-*clap*." *(count again using this pattern; the claps come on the multiples of two)*

"We counted by twos that time! Let's do it again!" *(repeat pattern, emphasizing multiples of two)*

"Now, it's time to eat the carrots! Yum yum yum!" *(make rabbit pretend to eat carrots)*

If desired, repeat the pattern with threes, fours, and fives. Make sure that you spread the carrots out so the children can see the multiples in each hole. Always ask the children to first identify how many carrots are in each hole, then count all the carrots, then repeat the numbers with the movement activity. Use these patterns for the movement, with the claps always emphasizing the number you are counting by:

Threes: snap fingers on one hand, snap fingers on other hand, *clap*

Fours: tap one foot, tap other foot, slap knees, *clap*

Fives: tap one foot, tap other foot, snap fingers on one hand, snap fingers on other hand, *clap*

End by having the bunny say:

"Thank you for helping me count all those carrots . . . but now I have a tummy ache!"

Variations

► If your group gets antsy or consists of mainly younger children, you may wish to end after counting by twos or threes.

► If you are working with older children, you can continue the pattern by counting by sixes, sevens, eights, nines, or tens. You may need to make larger background pieces to do this.

► If desired, give each child a turn to pick a carrot from the patch during the story.

► You can follow up the story with math problems—for example, "If there are two carrots in each hole, and there are five holes, how many carrots are there?" You may even wish to have the children place carrots in the holes and come up with their own math problems for the group. Make sure that you take the time to show the carrots in the holes, count to check answers, and use language such as: "There are two sticks in each hole, and there are five holes—2 times 5 equals 10." Exposing young children to mathematical terminology in context makes such terms less intimidating later on.

► This activity can also be used as a craft! Replace the felt with construction paper and invite the children to make their own carrot patches, then retell the story themselves.

IIA1, IIA4, IIA5, IIB1, IIB2, IIB3

97 *Chooky-Doodle-Doo* Flannelboard

Based on the book by Jan Whiten (Somerville, MA: Candlewick, 2014)

Five chicks and a rooster work together to pull a stubborn worm out of the dirt, only to find it is a shoelace attached to an old boot.

Attach two long pieces of string to the boot. When you begin the story, position the boot behind the dirt piece so that the end of a piece of string pokes up through the slit. As the chicks pull on the string, tug the boot up out of the hole.

IA1, IA2, IA3, IIA1

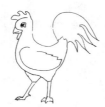

98 *Counting Candle Jumps* (adapted traditional)

Write the numbers 1 through 10 on index cards. Hold the cards face down and allow each child to select a card before taking a turn starring in the following rhyme. Place an unlit candle on the floor and have each child jump over the candle the designated number of times as you say the rhyme (using the child's name) and count together.

(Name) be nimble, (Name) be quick,
(Name) jump over the candlestick!
(Number) jumps is the right amount.
(Name) will jump while we all count!

IC2, IIA1, IIA3

More Entries Related to This Topic

Opposites

99 Opposite Action Rhyme

Act out the words as you say the rhyme.

Run and run and run as *fast* as you can,
Then move in *slow* motion and finally stand.
Shake your sillies out when I say *go*,
Then *stop* when I say whoa, whoa, whoa!

Raise your hands up *high* to the sky,
Then go *low* to the ground and sit with a sigh.

> **IC2**

More Entries Related to This Topic

Shapes

100 Can You Draw a Shape? (to the tune of "She'll Be Comin' 'Round the Mountain")

Pass out rhythm sticks and invite the children to draw each shape in the air with you as you sing the song.

Can you draw a square, draw a square?
Oh, can you draw a square, draw a square?
Draw a line and then three more,
They are all the same for sure.
Oh, can you draw a square, draw a square?

Can you draw a circle, draw a circle.
Oh, can you draw a circle, draw a circle?
A circle is round,
With no corners to be found.
Oh, can you draw a circle, draw a circle?

Can you draw a triangle, draw a triangle?
Oh, can you draw a triangle, draw a triangle?
Make one side and then make two,
Then make a third, that's all you do.
Oh, can you draw a triangle, draw a triangle?

> **IC2, IE5, IIE2, IIE4, IIE5**

101 Shape Song (to the tune of "Here We Go 'Round the Mulberry Bush")

A circle is a shape that goes 'round and 'round,
'Round and 'round,
'Round and 'round,

A circle is a shape that goes 'round and 'round
Which makes balls so fun!

A triangle is a shape with three sides,
Three sides,
Three sides,
A triangle is a shape with three sides,
Which makes it perfect for ice cream cones.

A square is shape where four sides are equal,
Four sides are equal,
Four sides are equal,
A square is a shape where four sides are equal,
Which makes a great house.

IIE2, IIE3, IIE4

102 **Square** (to the tune of "B-I-N-G-O")

I am a shape that has four equal sides
And square is my name, oh!
S-Q-U-A-R-E,
S-Q-U-A-R-E,
S-Q-U-A-R-E,
And square is my name, oh!

IC2, IIE2, IIE3, IIE4

Another Entry Related to This Topic

*Pumpkin Patch Match, p. 121

Size

103 *Can I Come Too?* **Flannelboard**

Based on the book by Brian Patten (Atlanta, GA: Peachtree, 2013)

A little mouse goes on a quest to see the biggest animal in the world and makes lots of friends along the way.

IA1, IA2, IA3, ID2

More Entries Related to This Topic

The Ant and the Crumb: A Folktale from Spain Flannelboard, p. 37

I'm the Biggest Thing in the Ocean Flannelboard, p. 26

Nesting Dolls, p. 134

Recommended Books

Big Bug by Henry Cole. New York: Little Simon, 2014.

Shape Capers by Cathryn Falwell. New York: Greenwillow, 2007.

Turtle Splash! Countdown at the Pond by Cathryn Falwell. New York: Greenwillow, 2001.

E-mergency! by Tom Lichtenheld. San Francisco, CA: Chronicle, 2011.

Hurry Up and Slow Down by Layn Marlow. New York: Holiday House, 2008.

The Tortoise and the Hare by Jerry Pinkney. New York: Little, Brown, 2013.

Opposites Everywhere: Sign Language for Opposites by Dawn Babb Prochovnic. Minneapolis, MN: Magic Wagon, 2012.

Sylvie by Jennifer Sattler. New York: Random House, 2009.

Square Cat by Elizabeth Schoonmaker. New York: Aladdin, 2011.

Green by Laura Vaccaro Seeger. New York: Roaring Brook Press, 2012.

8

Fairy Tales and Castles

- -

104 The Castle Gate

Have two children join their raised hands, "London Bridge"–style, so that the other children can pass through.

Walk through the castle gate
One by one, we can't be late.

Repeat until all the children have passed through.

Hop through the castle gate
One by one, we can't be late.

Repeat until all the children have passed through.

Crawl through the castle gate
One by one, we can't be late.

Repeat until all the children have passed through.

Tiptoe through the castle gate
One by one, we can't be late.

Repeat until all the children have passed through.

Walk through the castle gate
One by one, we can't be late.

Repeat, getting faster and faster.

You never know what the gate will do.
It might just close right on . . . you! *(the children playing the gate bring down their hands, "trapping" the child under the gate)*

      IC2, IE5

105 *Dragon, Dragon

Dragon, dragon, stomp around, *(stomp in place)*
Swish your tail up and down, *(shake bottoms)*
Unfold your wings, *(open arms wide)*
And fly so high, *(flap arms)*
And breathe your fire to the sky! *(blow upward)*

      IC2, IE5

106 Dragon Romp

Encourage the children to act out the words to this settling-down rhyme.

Dragon romp,
Dragon stomp,
Dragon cha-cha-cha.
Dragon dance,
Dragon prance,
Dragon la-la-la.
Dragon roar,
Dragon soar,
Dragon fly around.
Dragon slow,
Dragon low,
Dragon sit back down.

      IC2, IE5

107 *Fairy Dance (to the tune of "The Hokey Pokey")

Pass out rhythm sticks, chopsticks, or straws to use as fairy wands during the song.

You put your left wing in,
You put your left wing out,
You put your left wing in,
And shake it all about.
Do the fairy dance
And turn yourself around
And sprinkle some fairy dust!

You put your right wing in . . .
You put your wand in . . .

    IC2, IE5

108 Fairy-Tale Characters Know It (to the tune of "If You're Happy and You Know It")

If you're a princess and you know it, clap your hands!
If you're a princess and you know it, clap your hands!
If you're a princess and you know it, then your wave will surely show it,
    (princess wave)
If you're a princess and you know it, clap your hands!

If you're a troll and you know it, stomp your feet!
If you're a troll and you know it, stomp your feet!
If you're a troll and you know it, then your growl will surely show it, *(growl)*
If you're a troll and you know it, stomp your feet!

If you're a prince and you know it, shout "Huzzah!"
If you're a prince and you know it, shout "Huzzah!"
If you're a prince and you know it, then your smile will surely show it, *(smile big)*
If you're a prince and you know it, shout "Huzzah!"

    IC2

109 5 Brave Knights

5 knights so gallant and brave,
Had to enter a scary cave.
In the cave there was a dragon,
Which startled 1 knight, who fell into a wagon!

4 knights . . .
3 knights . . .
2 knights . . .

1 knight so gallant and brave,
Had to enter a scary cave.
In the cave there was a dragon,
But the brave knight waved a flag and
Soon the dragon charged the floor,
And the knight shoved him out the door!

    IC2, IIA1, IIA4

110   5 Frogs Need a Kiss

5 little frogs croaking so loud,
"Please kiss me," they called to the crowd.
A brave girl came forward and kissed 1 frog.
He croaked, "Not me," and hopped into the bog.

4 little frogs . . .
3 little frogs . . .
2 little frogs . . .

1 little frog croaking so loud,
"Please kiss me," he called to the crowd.
A brave girl came forward and kissed that frog.
And a prince arose from the swirling fog!

IC2, IIA1, IIA4, IIA5, IIB1

111   *5 Little Frogs

5 little frogs sitting by the pond,
Waiting for a fairy godmother to wave her magic wand.
Magic flew from the wand at night,
And 1 little frog jumped out of sight.

4 little frogs . . .
3 little frogs . . .
2 little frogs . . .

1 little frog sitting by the pond,
Waiting for a fairy godmother to wave her magic wand.
Magic flew from the wand at night,
And turned the frog into a prince, much to the princess's delight!

IC2, IIA1, IIA4, IIA5, IIB1

112   *5 Little Princesses

5 little princesses dancing at the ball,
"Where's my prince charming?" they all call.
One girl's daddy rushes through the door,
Then the music continues for the other 4.

4 little princesses dancing at the ball,
"Where's my prince charming?" they all call.
One girl's daddy arrives in time for tea,
Then the music continues for the other 3.

3 little princesses dancing at the ball,
"Where's my prince charming?" they all call.
One girl's daddy announces their dinner of stew,
Then the music continues for the other 2.

2 little princesses dancing at the ball,
"Where's my prince charming?" they both call.
One girl's daddy spins her until she is done,
Then the music continues for just 1.

1 little princess dancing at the ball,
"Where's my prince charming?" she calls.
Her daddy arrives with a bow and a rose,
And she dances home on her tippy toes.

IC2, IIA1, IIA4, IIA5, IIB1

113 *5 Tired Knights **Flannelboard**

Place the pieces on the board. Remove one knight at the end of each verse.

5 little knights at the end of the day,
Getting ready to hit the hay.
1 little knight rides his horse around the keep,
Gives a great big yawn, and goes to sleep.
Goodnight, Knight!

4 little knights . . .
3 little knights . . .
2 little knights . . .
1 little knight . . .

IC2, IIA1, IIA4, IIA5, IIB1

114 *Good Night, Knight* **Flannelboard**

Based on the book by Betsy Lewin (New York: Holiday House, 2015)

Knight has a dream about golden cookies, and he and his horse go on a quest to find them.

IA1, IA2, IA3

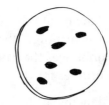

115 I Am a Giant

I am a giant, *stomp, stomp, stomp. (stomp feet)*
I eat up veggies with a *chomp, chomp, chomp. (extend arms and clap hands loudly)*
I eat till my belly fills with *more, more, more. (mime eating and show belly expanding)*
Then I fall asleep with a *snore, snore, snore. (rest head on joined hands and make loud snoring noises)*

     IC2

116 Magic Bean (to the tune of "Dreidel, Dreidel, Dreidel")

Act out the words as you sing the song.

I had a magic bean,
I buried it so deep.
I gave it sun and water,
And vines began to creep.

Oh, beanstalk, beanstalk, beanstalk,
Grow up to the sky.
Oh, beanstalk, beanstalk, beanstalk,
Now it's time to climb.

I stood up in the clouds,
I looked all around,
And when I saw a giant,
It was time to go back down.

Oh, beanstalk, beanstalk, beanstalk,
Now I'm climbing down,
Oh, beanstalk, beanstalk, beanstalk,
Help me to the ground.

Now the giant's coming,
I ran to get my ax,
I took it to the beanstalk,
And gave it twenty whacks!

Oh, beanstalk, beanstalk, beanstalk,
Falling to the ground,
Oh, beanstalk, beanstalk, beanstalk,
With a giant crashing sound.

     IC2, IE5

117 *****My Magic Wand** (to the tune of "And the Green Grass Grows All Around")

Use a drumstick, chopstick, or rhythm stick as a magic wand for this activity. If desired, have the children suggest motions for each verse.

My magic wand, it swishes like this,
With the prettiest swish that you ever did see.
And it makes you dance and dance and dance,
And the magic wand goes swish like this,
And the magic wand goes swish.

My magic wand, it swishes like this,
With the prettiest swish that you ever did see.
And it makes you jump and jump and jump,
And makes you dance and dance and dance,
And the magic wand goes swish like this,
And the magic wand goes swish.

Continue, adding more motions with each verse:

. . . and it makes you flap your arms like this . . .
. . . and it makes you wiggle your fingers like this . . .
. . . and it makes you spin and spin and spin . . .

End by having the magic wand make everyone sit back down.

IC2, IE5

118 *Oh No, Little Dragon!* **Flannelboard**

Based on the book by Jim Averbeck (New York: Atheneum, 2012)

Little Dragon accidentally loses his spark when he plays too wildly in the bathtub, but his mama's love puts the spark back in his heart. Use a spray bottle to spritz the children with water when Little Dragon splashes.

IA1, IA2, IA3

119 Rapunzel Rhyme

Rapunzel, Rapunzel high in her tower *(move hands upward to outline tower)*
Liked to sit and read books by the hour. *(mime reading a book)*
The prince said, "Come out!" but she didn't dare. *(make "come here" motion)*
It would take her all day just to braid her hair! *(mime braiding hair)*

      IC2

Recommended Books

Giant Dance Party by Betsy Bird. New York: Greenwillow, 2013.

Ten Big Toes and a Prince's Nose by Nancy Gow. New York: Sterling, 2010.

Very Little Red Riding Hood by Teresa Heapy. New York: Houghton Mifflin Harcourt, 2014.

Wilfred by Ryan Higgins. New York: Dial Books for Young Readers, 2013.

A Bean, a Stalk, and a Boy Named Jack by William Joyce. New York: Simon and Schuster, 2014.

Not Last Night But the Night Before by Colin McNaughton. Somerville, MA: Candlewick, 2009.

I Want a Party! by Tony Ross. Minneapolis, MN: Lerner, 2011.

Dragons Love Tacos by Adam Rubin. New York: Dial Books for Young Readers, 2012.

Goldilocks and the Three Dinosaurs by Mo Willems. New York: HarperCollins, 2012.

Princess Me by Karma Wilson. New York: Simon and Schuster, 2007.

9

Family and Friends

· ·

120 Are You My Friend? (to the tune of "Frère Jacques")

Are you my friend, are you my friend?
Please say yes, please say yes!
We can play all day, we can play all day,
Hip, hip, hooray! Hip, hip, hooray!

Here are my toys, here are my toys,
You can share, you can share!
You've brought some too, you've brought some too,
Let's start with teddy bears! Let's start with teddy bears!

      IC2

121 *Did You Ever See a Family? (to the tune of "Did You Ever See a Lassie?")

Did you ever see a mommy, a mommy, a mommy,
Did you ever see a mommy hug this way and that?
Hug this way and that way, and that way and this way?
Did you ever see a mommy hug this way and that?

Did you ever see a daddy, a daddy, a daddy,
Did you ever see a daddy kiss this way and that?

Kiss this way and that way, and that way and this way?
Did you ever see a daddy kiss this way and that?

Did you ever see a grandma, a grandma, a grandma,
Did you ever see a grandma tickle this way and that?
Tickle this way and that way, and that way and this way?
Did you ever see a grandma tickle this way and that?

> IC2

122 Family (to the tune of "B-I-N-G-O")

At home I have a family,
And I am really glad!
F-A-M-I-L-Y,
F-A-M-I-L-Y,
F-A-M-I-L-Y,
I live with mom and dad!

Continue, replacing one letter with a clap each time.

> IC2, IC3

123 Friends

1 little friend playing all alone
Caught a ball that was thrown!
2 little friends busy playing ball,
Saw another friend playing with a doll.
3 little friends start a jumping rhyme,
Another joins in and jumps in time.
4 little friends swing until dark,
Then it's time to leave the park.

> IC2, IE5, IIA1

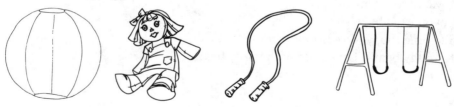

124 Garden Friends

On a sunny Saturday,
All of the insects came out to play.
A bee was buzzing all alone,
On a flower as tall as a throne.
A butterfly landed gracefully,
Flapping her wings for all to see.
A platoon of ants went marching by,

In search of crumbs from apple pie.
A ladybug was tending the leaves,
From the flower's little thieves.
All were happy to enjoy the day,
In the garden on this Saturday.

IC2

125 **Hello, My Friend** (to the tune of "Skip to My Lou")

Hello, my friend, how do you do?
Hello, my friend, how do you do?
Hello, my friend, how do you do?
How are you today?

Encourage the children to mill around shaking each other's hands as you sing the song. Then pause and tell them to find a friend and share their names. Resume the song and continue shaking hands, with as many name breaks as you like.

IE1, IE6

126 ***Little Blue Truck* Flannelboard**

Based on the book by Alice Schertle (New York: Harcourt, 2008)

A little blue truck finds his way out of trouble with the help of his animal friends.

IA1, IA2, IA3

127 ***Mommy, Mommy** (to the tune of "Twinkle, Twinkle Little Star")

Mommy, Mommy, here you are,
Always with me near and far.
You hug and kiss me every night,
And chase away any nighttime frights.
Mommy, Mommy, here you are,
Always with me near and far.

IC2

128 **Our House**

My family lives in our house,
It's a very special place.
When I wake up in the morning,
There's always a friendly face.
My daddy makes me breakfast,
My mommy ties my shoes.
My sister reminds me to brush my teeth,
And my brother knows what to do.
I love my dog, Fluffy,
He always wags his tail.
Fluffy greets me with big kisses,
Every day without fail.
When the moon has risen,
And it's time to go to bed,
We pile under our covers for stories,
And get goodnight kisses on our heads.

IC2, IE5

   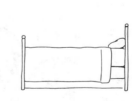

129 ***Row, Row Flannelboard** (traditional)

Row, row! A-fishing we'll go!
How many fishes have you, Joe?
"One for my father,
One for my mother,
One for my sister,
One for my brother,
And one for the little fisher boy!"
1, 2, 3, 4, 5!

IC2, IIA1

130 Sharing

Teach the American Sign Language sign SHARE and sign it as you say this rhyme.

Sharing is nice to do,
With your friends and family too!
I like to share my cookies and chips,
And my friend shares her toy ships.
We play and share all through the day,
That's how we know true friends we'll stay!

IC2

131 *Soon* Flannelboard

Based on the book by Timothy Knapman (Somerville, MA: Candlewick, 2015)

A little elephant named Raju goes on an adventure with his mother.

Make sure to have the children help you act out the mother elephant's actions as she scares each of the other animals away.

IA1, IA2, IA3

132 *Who's Next Door?* Prop Story

Based on the book by Mayuko Kishira and Jun Takabatake (Berkeley, CA: Owlbooks, 2011)

Chicken is excited when someone new moves in next door, but he's puzzled when he never sees his new neighbor. Turns out it's Owl, and it's not until Chicken stays up late and Owl gets up early that they finally cross paths.

This story makes a delightful puppet play. Decorate two similar-size boxes as houses and use Chicken and Owl puppets to tell the story. Make large versions of the notes that the two friends write to one another and invite the children to help the characters read them. Set up a whiteboard, chalkboard, or flipchart between the houses at the end of the story. Extend the story by asking the children what kind of messages they think the two friends would write to one another. If your group is older, invite participants to help write on the board or paper.

IA1, IA2, IA3

133 Windy Moves

My friend and I went out to play,
On a very windy day.
We flapped our arms back and forth,
And pretended to fly north. *(flap arms)*
Once we landed we ran so fast,
But the wind went sailing past. *(run in place)*
We raised our arms to fly a kite,
But the wind lifted it to new heights. *(lift arms)*
When the wind finally settled down,
We had our picnic on the ground. *(sit down)*

IC2

More Entries Related to This Topic

Mother's Day: Johnny Sparkit Went to Market Flannelboard, p. 106

Party Hats Flannelboard, p. 101

*Seesaw: A Partner Rhyme, p. 135

*The Seesaw Flannelboard, p. 135

Swing Step, p. 152

Telephone Rhyme, p. 136

*Two Little Monkeys Puppet Story, p. 28

What Do I See at Home? Flannelboard, p. 48

Recommended Books

Hello My Name Is Bob by Linas Alsenas. New York: Scholastic, 2009.

Time Together: Me and Dad by Maria Catherine. North Mankato, MN: Picture Window Books, 2014.

Little Eliot, Big City by Mike Curato. New York: Henry Holt, 2014.

Mommy Hugs by Karen Katz. New York: Simon and Schuster, 2006.

Who Wants a Hug? by Jeff Mack. New York: HarperCollins, 2015.

Meet Me at the Moon by Gianna Marino. New York: Viking, 2013.

Quick, Slow, Mango! by Anik McGrory. New York: Bloomsbury, 2011.

Puddle Pug by Kim Norman. New York: Sterling, 2014.

Hip, Hip, Hooray! It's Family Day! Sign Language for Family by Dawn Babb Prochovnic. Minneapolis, MN: Magic Wagon, 2012.

Alex and Lulu: Two of a Kind by Lorena Siminovich. Somerville, MA: Candlewick, 2008.

10
Food

134 *Apples Big and Apples Small

Apples big *(spread arms wide)*
And apples small *(hold hands close together to show a small apple)*
Clap your hands *(clap hands)*
And eat them all! *(mime eating)*

. . . wiggle your fingers and eat them all!
. . . dance around and eat them all!
. . . jump up and down and eat them all!
. . . tap your knees and eat them all!
. . . touch your toes and eat them all!
. . . turn around and eat them all!
. . . sit back down and eat them all!

Replace "apples" to make this rhyme fit other themes—for example, "watermelon" for a summer-themed program, "latkes" for a Hanukkah-themed program, or "waffles" for a morning-themed program.

IC2, IE5

135 Bananas Flannelboard

1 banana, 2 banana, 3 banana, 4,
Hanging on the banana tree by my door.
5 banana, 6 banana, 7 banana, 8,
The hungry little monkeys watch from the gate.
9 banana, 10 banana, I pick them and then,
I say, "Time for dinner, monkey friends! Come on in!"
In come the monkeys, 1 and 2.
With 10 bananas, what should we do?
You see, my friends, we are not done yet—
How many bananas does each monkey get?

Encourage the children to brainstorm ways to divide the bananas. Some children may answer "Each monkey gets five bananas!" and may say that 10 divided by 2 is 5. Even if this happens, take the time to count out the bananas one at a time for each monkey and count up the sets to show that each monkey gets five.

IC2, IE5, IIA1, IIA4, IIA5, IIA6, IIB1, IIB2, IIC1

136 Cake Chant

Cake, cake,
Put it on my plate!
It will taste so yummy,
While it goes to my tummy!
Cake, cake,
There's nothing as great!
A big piece of cake,
And the icing on my plate!

IC2

137 Cookout Beanbag Rhyme

This is a fun beanbag activity for food- or summer-themed storytimes. As a bonus, when you are moving the hamburger from hand to hand in the first part of the rhyme, you are also signing HAMBURGER in American Sign Language.

Hold the beanbag in your right hand. Hold your left hand facing up. Turn your right hand over to deposit the beanbag into your left palm. Then turn both hands and repeat the motion the other way, as if you are shaping a hamburger patty. Repeat this motion rhythmically through the first verse.

I'm making a HAMBURGER for the grill.
Will I eat it? Yes, I will!

Place the beanbag on your flat left palm. Use your right hand as a spatula to lift the beanbag and flip it over. Then switch hands. Repeat this motion throughout verse two.

I'm flipping my HAMBURGER on the grill.
Will I eat it? Yes, I will!

Hold the beanbag in your left palm. Pretend to squirt on ketchup, mustard, and the like with your other hand.

Now I'm fixing my HAMBURGER from the grill.
Will I eat it? Yes, I will!

Place the beanbag in your left hand. Sign EAT by raising the beanbag toward your mouth, then placing the beanbag in your right hand. Repeat with the right hand.

Now I'm EATING my hamburger. This is fun!
Did I EAT it? Yes, all done!

If desired, sign ALL DONE or FINISH at the end.

IC2, IE5

138 **Cookin' in the Kitchen Flannelboard** (to the tune of "Someone's in the Kitchen")

Someone's in the kitchen with mama,
Someone's in the kitchen I know-o-o-o.
Someone's in the kitchen with mama,
Eating the mangos!

Someone, someone,
Who could that someone be-ee-ee?
Someone, someone,
Ooh, that someone is me!

. . . eating the Cheerios!
. . . eating the nachos!
. . . eating the pistachios!
. . . eating the tacos!
. . . eating the burritos!
. . . eating the Jell-O!

IC2, IE5

139 Donuts Flannelboard

6 sprinkled donuts in the bakery bag,
Waiting until we get home will be such a drag.
No one will notice if I eat just one,
I gobble it down to the very last crumb!

5 sprinkled donuts . . .
4 sprinkled donuts . . .
3 sprinkled donuts . . .
2 sprinkled donuts . . .

1 sprinkled donut in the bakery bag,
Waiting until we get home will be such a drag.
No one will notice if I eat just one,
I gobble it down until they are all *gone!*

No sprinkled donuts in the bakery bag,
I confess to my parents as my shoulders sag.
My parents turn the car around,
We'll order more donuts at the bakery in town!

IC2, IIA1, IIA4, IIA5, IIB1

140 *Eating Song (to the tune of "Frère Jacques")

Sign the words in capital letters as you sing the song.

EATING APPLES,
EATING APPLES,
Yum yum yum. *(rub stomach)*

Yum yum yum. *(rub stomach)*
APPLES are DELICIOUS,
APPLES are DELICIOUS,
In my tum. *(point to stomach)*
In my tum.

Repeat with other foods (bananas, bread, carrots, crackers, grapes, ice cream, pizza).

IC2, IE5

141 *Going on a Picnic Flannelboard

Pass out the food items to the children. Invite the children to put the items in the basket on the flannelboard as you call them out.

I'm going on a picnic, a-tisket, a-tasket.
I'll bring an apple in my picnic basket!

Repeat with other food items.

Now it's time to go out, a-tisket, a-tasket.
Look at all the yummy food in my picnic basket!

IC2, IE5, IID3

142 Grapes

Grapes, grapes, yummy and sweet *(rub tummy)*
A bunch of grapes is my favorite treat. *(sign GRAPES)*
Some are red and some are green, *(sign RED and GREEN)*
Some the deepest purple you've ever seen. *(sign PURPLE)*
Grapes can be small or *(hunch into a ball)*
Grapes can be big. *(spread arms wide)*
They grow on a vine so you don't have to dig. *(mime picking grapes from a vine)*
Pick one grape or pick a bunch
Let's all have some grapes for lunch! *(sign GRAPES)*

grape

IC2, IE5

red

green

purple

143 My Grocery List (to the tune of "When the Saints Go Marching In")

Use a chalkboard, whiteboard, or piece of flipchart paper to brainstorm with the children a list of twelve items that might be found at the grocery store. If your group is older, you may wish to have the children write the items themselves, for writing practice. With younger groups, write the items yourself, spelling out each word as you do so.

Use a real clock or a paper clock made from the template provided to change the time with each verse.

At 1 o'clock *(point to clock)*
I ran to the store *(run in place)*
And said, "Do you have any _____?" *(point to item on list)*
The lady said, "No."
I was so sad. *(make sad face)*
So I ran back home again. *(run in place)*

At 2 o'clock . . .
At 3 o'clock . . .
At 4 o'clock . . .
At 5 o'clock . . .
At 6 o'clock . . .
At 7 o'clock . . .
At 8 o'clock . . .
At 9 o'clock . . .
At 10 o'clock . . .
At 11 o'clock . . .

At 12 o'clock *(point to clock)*
I ran to the store *(run in place)*
And said, "Do you have any _____?" *(point to item on list)*
The lady said, "Go to sleep!"
So I did.
Zzzzzzzzzz. *(mime sleeping)*

      IC2, IE5, IIA1

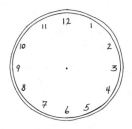

144 **Popcorn Rhyme**

Oil, oil in the pot *(mime pouring oil in pot)*
Wait till it gets nice and hot.
Pour the popcorn kernels in *(mime pouring popcorn in pot)*
And soon the popping will begin.
First a pop *(jump up on each pop)*
And then a *pop pop*
Then *pop pop pop pop pop!*
Then a stop!
Pour the popcorn from the pot, *(mime pouring popcorn into bowl)*
Add salt and butter—careful, it's hot! *(shake imaginary salt on)*
Take a handful, it's a treat. *(mime taking a handful)*
Now at last it's time to eat! *(pretend to eat the popcorn)*

      IC2, IE5

145 **Stir It Up!**

Act out the words as you say the rhyme.

Bubble, bubble,
Pop, pop, pop,
The oil in the pan is
Hot, hot, hot.

We'll add our meat,
Sizzle, sizzle, sizzle,
Stir with our spoon and
Add sauce with a drizzle.

Next we'll add the broccoli
Because it's a bright green,
Cover the pot
And let it steam.

Salt and pepper,
Shake, shake, shake,
A few more minutes
Is all it should take.

Hot rice or steaming noodles
In the bottom of the bowl,
Stir fry chicken on the top,
Along with a crunchy egg roll!
Crunch!

      IC2, IE5

146 *Waffle Song Flannelboard (to the tune of "I Love My Rooster")

Waffles are yummy, my favorite food.
I eat them up when I'm in the mood.
And I top my waffles with butter and syrup,
Yum-yum-yummy, yum-yummy, yum-yummy, yum.

Waffles are yummy, my favorite food.
I eat them up when I'm in the mood.
And I top my waffles with strawberries,
And I top my waffles with butter and syrup,
Yum-yum-yummy, yum-yummy, yum-yummy, yum.

Continue adding other toppings to the song as you add the pieces to the board. End by asking the children to sing the whole song as fast as they can!

IC2, IE5

147 Watermelon Flannelboard

Watermelon, watermelon juicy and sweet,
How many slices can I eat?
1, 2, 3, 4, 5! (*place watermelon slices on the board*)
Watermelon, watermelon spit the seeds,
This is quite a silly deed!
1, 2, 3, 4, 5! (*place watermelon
    seeds in the bucket*)

IC2, IE5, IIA1

More Entries Related to This Topic

Recommended Books

Rainbow Stew by Cathryn Falwell. New York: Lee and Low, 2013.

Community Soup by Alma Fullerton. Toronto, ON: Pajama Press, 2013.

Badger's Fancy Meal by Keiko Kasza. New York: Putnam, 2007.

Eat Up, Little Donkey by Rindert Kromhout and Annemarie van Haeringen. Wellington, NZ: Gecko, 2013.

Night of the Veggie Monster by George McClements. New York: Bloomsbury, 2008.

The Case of the Missing Donut by Alison McGhee. New York: Dial, 2013.

Jack and the Jelly Bean Stalk by Rachel Mortimer. Wilton, CT: Tiger Tales, 2014.

The Watermelon Seed by Greg Pizzoli. New York: Disney/Hyperion Books, 2013.

Secret Pizza Party by Adam Rubin. New York: Dial Books for Young Readers, 2013.

Food Trucks! by Mark Todd. Boston, MA: Houghton Mifflin Harcourt, 2014.

11

Holidays and Celebrations

· ·

Birthdays

148 Birthday

Today is your birthday, it's a great day indeed.
Your family, who loves you, all have agreed. *(nod head)*
Today is your day, so do what you will,
Scream from the rooftops or roll down a hill. *(raise hands overhead)*
Whatever you choose, just remember this,
We wish you a year that is full of bliss! *(mime hug)*

>   **IC2, IE5**

149 Birthday Surprise

Act out the words as you say the rhyme.

I'm going to bake a birthday cake,
As tall as a tower,
And on the very top,
I'll place a pretty flower.

The tower is tilting a little,
Some icing will surely help,
Oooh, the cake's still hot,
Uh-oh, the icing is starting to melt.
Dad helps me steady the cake,
We start to sing a tune,
Happy Birthday, Mommy,
We love you from here to the moon!

      IC2, IE5

150 *Candle Rhyme

Teach the sign CANDLE to use in this rhyme.

Candle, candle burning bright, *(sign CANDLE)*
Lighting up the darkest night.
Thank you for your shining light,
But with one puff, you're out of sight. *(blow on the fingers representing the flames
    and curl them into a fist to show the candle going out)*

      IC2, IE5

candle

151 How Many Candles Flannelboard

5 shining candles on the birthday cake.
How many puffs will it take?
I make my wish and give a great big blow,
And smile while the crowd says, "Go, go, go!"

4 shining candles . . .
3 shining candles . . .
2 shining candles . . .

1 shining candle on the birthday cake.
How many puffs will it take?
I make my wish and give a great big blow,
And smile while the crowd cheers, "Way to go!"

      IC2, IIA1, IIA4, IIA5, IIB1

152 Party Hats Flannelboard

The table is set with snacks and cake,
5 party hats are out for my guests to take.
Billy arrives first and knocks on the door,
He takes a party hat and then there are 4.
When Jenny arrives she squeals with glee,
She takes a party hat and then there are 3.
Jake rushes in all dressed in blue,
He grabs a matching party hat and then there are 2.
Sally arrives, blowing big bubbles with her gum,
She takes a party hat and then there is 1.
I take the last hat, I'm ready for fun,
All my guests are here, the party has begun!

IC2, IIA1, IIA4, IIA5, IIB1

Fall Holidays

153 5 Jack-O-Lanterns Flannelboard

5 Jack-O-Lanterns on the windowsill,
The wind blew 1 candle out, causing quite a chill.
4 Jack-O-Lanterns on the windowsill,
A ghost went by and said "*Boo*," scaring 1 so he rolled downhill.
3 Jack-O-Lanterns on the windowsill,
A mummy asked if they wanted pumpkin pie, leaving 1 feeling ill.
2 Jack-O-Lanterns on the windowsill,
A witch pointed her finger at them and 1 is frozen still.
1 Jack-O-Lantern alone on the windowsill,
Halloween is his favorite holiday, tonight was a thrill!

IC2, IIA1, IIA4, IIA5, IIB1

154 5 Little Pilgrims Flannelboard

5 little pilgrims on Thanksgiving Day,
Came together to say thanks and pray.
The first pilgrim said, "Look at this dinner!"
The second broke the wishbone to see the winner.
The third pilgrim said, "I see pumpkin pie."
The fourth said, "Yummy, so do I!"
The fifth pilgrim couldn't eat another bite,
So they went to bed with a "Goodnight!"

IC2, IIA1, IIA4, IIA5, IIB1

Winter Holidays

155 *Getting Ready for the Holidays: A Parachute Story

Start by laying out the parachute on the floor and having the parents and children crouch by the edge. Explain that they will help tell the story with the parachute and must listen for the movements.

Once upon a time there was a little girl named Annie. When she was very small, she
  wasn't allowed to help decorate for the holidays. But then she grew up.
She got taller, *(lift parachute to knee height)*
and taller, *(lift parachute to waist height)*
and taller. *(lift parachute to shoulder height)*
She loved getting ready for the holidays, even though it was a very busy time.
  (move parachute back and forth quickly)
She loved decorating the house. She would put decorations way down low
  (move parachute to floor)
and way up high. *(lift parachute high)*
She would pop lots of popcorn to make popcorn strings! *(move parachute to waist
  height and wiggle it quickly up and down like popcorn popping)*
And when she wanted it to snow, she would sing her favorite song, "Jingle Bells."
  (sing "Jingle Bells" while "jingling" the parachute)
On the night before her big family celebration, Annie got under the covers.
  *(adults hold up the parachute and children go underneath; bring down the
  parachute to make a house)*
She went to sleep and she snored! *(encourage kids to snore)*
Then in the morning, when she woke up . . . *(adults lift parachute up high;
  encourage children to stand and stretch)*
. . . it was snowing! *(gently drift parachute downward)*
She went outside to see the snow. *(children return to edges of parachute)*
It snowed all day. *(dump cotton balls or pom-poms into the parachute and move it
  up and down to represent snow)*
When her family came over, she played in the snow and had a snowball fight.
  (move parachute quickly up and down)

But then she got tired. *(move parachute more slowly)*
She waved good-bye to her family, and gave a great big yawn! *(lift parachute up high)*
Then she settled down into bed. *(lower parachute to the floor)*
What a celebration!

> **IE5**

156 Little Latkes

Little latkes, little latkes,
Sizzle and pop,
Fry them in the pan,
Until they're crispy and hot!
Flip them once,
Till they're golden brown,
Put them on the plate,
And eat them right down!

> **IC2, IE5**

157 *I'm a Little Reindeer (to the tune of "I'm a Little Teapot")

I'm a little reindeer, watch me fly.
Hear my jingle bells as I go by.
Every year I help pull Santa's sleigh,
Here we go, up, up, and away!

> **IC2, IE5**

158 Kwanzaa (to the tune of "B-I-N-G-O")

Place the kinara on the board and point to a candle for each verse.

For 7 days we celebrate
This special festival.
7 principles,
7 candles,
7 days of love,
And Kwanzaa is its name, oh.

Refrain:
K-W-A-N-Z-A-A,
K-W-A-N-Z-A-A,
K-W-A-N-Z-A-A,
And Kwanzaa is its name, oh.

The first principle is *umoja* (oo-MOH-ja),
That means unity.
The second principle is *kujichagulia* (koo-jee-cha-goo-LEE-yah),

That means self-determination.
The third principle is *ujima* (oo-JEE-mah),
That means collective work and responsibility.
The fourth principle is *ujamaa* (oo-JAH-ma),
That means cooperative economics.
The fifth principle is *nia* (nee-AH),
That means a sense of purpose.
The sixth principle is *kuumba* (koo-OOM-bah),
That means creativity.
The seventh principle is *imani* (ee-MAH-nee),
That means faith.

IC2, IC3, IE5

159 **5 Candy Hearts Flannelboard**

5 candy hearts on Valentine's Day,
5 candy hearts with something special to say.
The first one said, "I love you, dear."
The second one said, "Come and sit near."
The third one said, "Please be mine."
The fourth one said, "You look fine!"
The fifth one said, "You're so sweet."
Then I took a bite of my candy treat.

IC2, IIA1, IIA4, IIA5

Spring Holidays

160 **Egg Hunt Flannelboard**

We're going on an egg hunt,
We're going to find a big one,
It will be filled with candy,
What a beautiful day!
Oh look! A field of flowers!
Can't go over it,
Can't go under it,
Can't go around it,
Got to go through it!

Oh look! A stream . . . Got to swim through it!
Oh look! A tree . . . Got to climb up it!
Oh look! A basket . . . Let's climb into it!

There's a beautiful egg!
And . . . uh-oh, a big bunny!

Quick, climb out of the basket,
Climb down the tree,
Swim through the stream,
And run through the field of flowers,
Until we get home!
Whew!
Crack open the egg, gobble up the candy,
And peek out the door.
Uh-oh! *(place small bunny on flannelboard)*

IE1, IE5

---

161 ***5 Pots of Gold Flannelboard**

5 pots of gold on this St. Patrick's Day.
Little Leprechaun gave one to his mommy, and what did she say?
"Thank you, Little Leprechaun!"
Now count with me, how many pots of gold do you see?

4 pots of gold . . . gave one to his daddy . . .
3 pots of gold . . . gave one to his brother . . .
2 pots of gold . . . gave one to his sister . . .
1 pot of gold . . . gave one to *you* . . .

IC2, IIA1, IIA4, IIA5, IIB1

---

162 ***10 Green Shamrocks Flannelboard** (to the tune of "10 Green Bottles")

10 green shamrocks growing on my lawn.
10 green shamrocks growing on my lawn.
And if I give 1 shamrock to a leprechaun,
There'll be 9 green shamrocks growing on my lawn.

Repeat, counting down to zero.

IC2, IIA1, IIA4, IIA5, IIB1

163 Mother's Day: Johnny Sparkit Went to Market Flannelboard

Write various prices from 1 to 10 cents on small sticky notes. Place the ten pennies on the bottom of the flannelboard. Place the other items on the top of the board and place a sticky note with a price under each one. Begin by inviting the children to help you count the pennies, then say the rhyme.

Johnny Sparkit went to market, 10 pennies in his fist.
He looked around until he found the perfect Mother's Day gift.
He said, "That's it! But I admit, I feel a little lost.
I could sing! The flower's the thing. But oh, how much does it cost?"

Ask the children to identify the price of the flower. Then ask questions, such as the following:

- ▶ Does Johnny have enough money to buy the flower?
- ▶ If he buys it, how much money will he have left?
  (count pennies together to verify)
- ▶ Does he have enough money left to buy something else, too?
  Which items can he afford?
- ▶ Which item costs the most? Which costs the least?

Repeat the rhyme until Johnny cannot buy anything else. This activity can also be used for Father's Day, a birthday, or any gift-giving holiday.

IIA1, IIA4, IIA5, IIA6, IIB1, IIB2

More Entries Related to This Topic

Recommended Books

Winter Candle by Jeron Ashford. Berkeley, CA: Creston Books, 2014.

Happy Birthday Madame Chapeau by Andrea Beaty. New York: Abrams, 2014.

The Twelve Days of Christmas by Jane Cabrera. New York: Holiday House, 2013.

A Year Full of Holidays by Susan Middleton Enya. New York: Putnam, 2010.

Gobble, Gobble by Cathryn Falwell. Nevada City, CA: Dawn Publications, 2011.

At the Old Haunted House by Helen Ketteman. New York: Two Lions, 2014.

Balloons Balloons Balloons by Dee Lillegard. New York: Dutton, 2007.

Meet Our Flag, Old Glory by April Jones Prince. New York: Little, Brown, 2004.

*Dinosaur vs. Santa by Bob Shea. New York: Hyperion, 2012.

*Here Comes the Easter Cat by Deborah Underwood. New York: Dial, 2014.

*I Love Birthdays by Anna Walker. New York: Simon and Schuster, 2010.

12

The Natural World

Dinosaurs

164 *Dinosaur, Dinosaur

Act out the words as you say the rhyme.

Dinosaur, Dinosaur, bounce around,
Dinosaur, Dinosaur, stomp the ground,
Dinosaur, Dinosaur, reach up high,
Some dinosaurs could even fly!

> IC2

165 Fossil Hunter

I am a fossil hunter,
I carry my pick and pail.
I dig through the rocks,
Looking for a dinosaur tale.

Tap, tap, tap,
Gently chipping off the stone.

Brush, brush, brush,
Beneath the rubble is a bone.

I lift away my discovery,
I'll be famous now.
At show-and-tell tomorrow,
All the kids will say wow!

IC2

Night and Day

166 *Night and Day Flannelboard Game** (to the tune of "The Farmer in the Dell")

Some things belong with night,
Some things belong with day.
Let's play a game—can you decide
What goes with night and day?

Place the sun and moon on top of the flannelboard.

We see the moon at night,
The sun's up in the day.
Let's play a game to see what else
Goes with the night and day.

Hold up the other objects and invite the children to place them on the correct side of the flannelboard—items that belong in the day go under the sun, items that belong in the night go under the moon.

IC2, IE5

167 Under the Nighttime Sky

Under the nighttime sky we pitch our tents,
Get our backpacks and check their contents.
We make a fire, and sing camp songs,
And soon everyone is singing along.
We strum and laugh all through the night,
Then an owl screeches and gives us a fright.
As the sky turns black, we put away our guitars,
Then make a wish on a shooting star.

IC2, IE5

168 *Wow! Said the Owl* Flannelboard

Based on the book by Tim Hopgood (New York: Farrar, Straus and Giroux, 2009)

A little owl stays awake through the day and marvels at all the colors of the world.

IA1, IA2, IA3

Another Entry Related to This Topic

*5 Little Stars, p. 50

▬▬

Trees

169 **Maple Song** (to the tune of "My Country, 'Tis of Thee")

I wish that I could be
A tall, tall maple tree *(hold arms up high to be a tree)*
With leaves so green.
And on a windy day *(sway arms like branches in the wind)*
See how my branches sway
And everyone would say
"That tree is keen!"

IC2

170 **Tree Rhyme**

How I'd like to be a tree *(hold arms up over head)*
Bending in the wind. *(move arms side to side)*
In spring I'd grow my buds just so *(hold arm out like a branch and make "bud" open
    on it with fingers of other hand)*
And birds would be my friends.
In summertime, I'd feel so fine *(shake hands like leaves)*
With leaves so full and green.
Autumn would come, time for fun—
My leaves the prettiest colors you've seen. *(hold spread hands out like leaves)*
They'd start to fall, but that's not all, *(make hands drift down to show leaves falling)*
Though winter time is here,
My branches are bare, but don't be scared—*(hold arms out at angles like bare
    branches)*
Spring comes every year!

IC2

▬▬

Weather

171 ***Cloud Song** (to the tune of "Frère Jacques")

See the clouds,
See the clouds,
In the sky,

In the sky,
White and fluffy clouds,
White and fluffy clouds,
Floating by.
Floating by.

See the clouds,
See the clouds,
Dark and gray,
Dark and gray,
When you see those clouds,
When you see those clouds,
Rainy day.
Rainy day.

       IC2, IE5

172 ***Raining on Me** (to the tune of "If You're Happy and You Know It")

Give an eyedropper, a small cup half-filled with water, and a tissue to each child. This activity works especially well for parent-child storytimes! Invite kids to drop ten "raindrops" on their hands, counting aloud together. Then sing the following song as each child drips the rain on the body part mentioned.

It's raining on my head, on my head.
It's raining on my head, on my head.
Oh, how I dread all this rain on my head.
It's raining on my head, on my head.

It's raining on my arm . . . it's not doing any harm, all this rain on my arm . . .
It's raining on my leg . . . help me, I beg, with this rain on my leg . . .
It's raining on my tummy . . . it isn't very funny, all this rain on my tummy . . .
It's raining on my grown-up . . . I really have to own up that it's raining on
    my grown-up . . .

       IC2, IIA1

173 ***Thunder Storm Action Rhyme**

Tap, tap, *(tap fingers on floor)*
Boom, boom, *(stomp feet on floor)*
The rain will be here soon.

Tap, tap, *(tap fingers on floor)*
Boom, boom, *(stomp feet on floor)*
It's a thunderstorm in June.

Tap, tap, *(tap fingers on floor)*
Boom, boom, *(stomp feet on floor)*
The lightning's lighting up the room!

Tap, tap, *(tap fingers on floor)*
Boom, boom, *(stomp feet on floor)*
The thunder shakes with a *Kaboom!*

Tap, tap, *(tap fingers on floor)*
Boom, boom, *(stomp feet on floor)*
Distant rumblings, rain like a monsoon.

Tap, tap, *(quietly tap fingers on floor)*
Boom, boom, *(quietly stomp feet on floor)*
Drizzle, drizzle.
I see the moon.

IC2, IE5

More Entries Related to This Topic

5 Boats Flannelboard, p. 162
Windy Moves, p. 84

▬▬▬

Winter

174 ***Hot Cocoa** (to the tune of "Frère Jacques")

Hot cocoa,
Hot cocoa,
In a mug,
In a mug.
When the weather's cold, I
Love to drink it up.
Glug, glug, glug.
Glug, glug, glug.

IC2, IE5

175 ***Little Hungry Bears**

1 little bear getting ready for winter,
Eating lots of blueberries with a chew, chew, chew.
Along came another friend who was hungry
And then there were 2.

2 little bears getting ready for winter,
Eating all the fruit that dropped from a tree.
Along came another friend who was hungry
And then there were 3.

3 little bears getting ready for winter,
They ate all the fruit and were looking for more.
Along came another friend who was hungry
And then there were 4.

4 little bears getting ready for winter,
Wandering around they spied honey in a hive.
Along came another friend who was hungry
And then there were 5.

5 friends eating their fill of honey,
When the bees swarmed out of the hive.
5 friends started running,
The bees behind them buzzing "Good-bye!"

IC2, IIA1, IIA4, IIA5

---

176 *Sledding Song (to the tune of "We're Going to Kentucky")

Have each child sit on a carpet square "sled" as you act out this song.

We're sledding down the hill,
We're sledding very fast,
We're leaning to the left and right
As the wind flies past.

We're bumping down the hill . . .

IC2, IE5

---

177 *Snowman, Snowman

Snowman, snowman, turn around.
Snowman, snowman, touch the ground.
Snowman, snowman, jump up high.
Snowman, snowman, make the snow fly.
Snowman, snowman, run, run, run.
Snowman, snowman, here's the sun.
Snowman, snowman, sway, sway, sway.
Snowman, snowman, melt away!

IC2, IE5

More Entries Related to This Topic

Spring

178 Butterfly Beanbag Rhyme

Give each child a beanbag. On each line, move both hands from sides to up in the air above your head. Each time your hands go above your head, pass the beanbag to the opposite hand. This activity may also be done with scarves.

Butterfly
In the sky
Flap your wings
And up you fly.
Back and forth,
To and fro,
Up, up, up,
And away you go!

Repeat several times, gradually increasing the speed of the rhyme and movements.

IC2, IE5

179 In My Garden Flannelboard

Hand out the vegetable shapes to the children and invite them to place the correct vegetable on the board when you say it in the rhyme.

In neat rows I plant my seeds,
Water them well and remove all weeds.
With sun and love my seeds will grow,
Into tasty treats we know!
Rows upon rows of veggies for me!
What's ready to eat, what do I see?

In neat rows I plant my seeds,
Water them well and remove all weeds.
With sun and love my seeds will grow,
Into tasty treats we know!
Rows upon rows of lettuce for me!
What's ready to eat, what do I
    see?

. . . carrots . . .
. . . green beans . . .
. . . strawberries . . .
. . . tomatoes . . .
. . . cucumbers . . .

IC2, IE5

180 *Seed Song (to the tune of "The Farmer in the Dell")

Here's a little seed, *(curl into a ball)*
Here's a little seed,
It's small and brown and in the ground,
It is a little seed.

The sun begins to shine, *(hold arms over head in a circle)*
The sun begins to shine,
It shines upon that little seed,
The sun begins to shine.

The rain begins to fall, *(move fingers in downward motion to represent rain)*
The rain begins to fall,
It falls upon that little seed,
The rain begins to fall.

The seed now starts to grow, *(slowly stand to represent seed growing)*
The seed now starts to grow,
Now it becomes a seedling.
The seed now starts to grow.

The leaves start to unfurl, *(turn hands over to represent leaves)*
The leaves start to unfurl,
It's become a little plant,
The leaves start to unfurl.

The flower opens up, *(spread arms wide)*
The flower opens up,
The flower says, "Hello, world!"
The flower opens up.

      IC2, IE5

181 Spring

Sunshine on my face, *(turn face toward sky)*
Wind in my hair, *(hold up hair)*
Birds fly in the sky, *(flap arms)*
I run without a care! *(run in place)*
Rows of flowers in place, *(pretend to pick a flower)*
Blades of grass have turned green, *(pretend to push lawnmower)*
Leaves opening in the trees, *(stand like a tree)*
The spring season is the new scene! *(cheer!)*

      IC2, IE5

More Entries Related to This Topic

Summer

182 The County Fair (to the tune of "Take Me Out to the Ballgame")

Take me out to the fair,
Take me out with the crowd,
Buy me some ice cream and funnel cakes,
I don't care how long it takes.
Let me moo, moo, moo with the cows,
And crow with the roosters,
For it's one, two, three days of fun
At the county fair!

IC2, IE5

183 I Found a Seashell

I found a little seashell,
In the deep blue sea.
It tumbled and it floated,
In the waves right up to me.
I held it in my hands,
And right up to my ear.
It sang an ocean tune,
That only I could hear!

IC2

184 *I Took a Walk on the Beach One Day Flannelboard / Prop Song
(to the tune of "I Took a Walk to Town One Day")

I took a walk on the beach one day,
And met a fish along the way.
And what do you think that fish did say?
Glub-Glub-Glub.

. . . and met a seagull along the way . . . *Awk-Awk-Awk.*
. . . and met a crab along the way . . . *Pinch-Pinch-Pinch.*

IC2, IE5

185 Ocean in a Bag Craft

Materials needed: resealable sandwich bags, craft sand, prepared blue gelatin, seashells, small plastic sea creatures or gummy fish

Directions:

1. Place sand in the bottom of the bag.

2. Add gelatin to the bag and crumble it to make it look like gel.

3. Add seashells and sea creatures to bag.

4. Carefully close the bag, making sure to let the excess air out.

5. Move the seashells and sea creatures around as desired in the bag.

186 Summertime

Summer is the greatest,
We're finally out of school.
We get to play all day,
And splash in the pool.

Sometimes we climb the mountains,
And float down a river,
We sing by the campfire,
When the moon is just a sliver.

Slowly licking ice cream cones,
And sweet treats made of ice,
Summer really is the best,
Being with friends and family is so nice.

IC2

187 **Summertime Market**

"Come along!" our mama calls,
We need to visit the produce stalls. *(wave people over)*
"Ripe melons!" "Strawberries!" "Corn in the husk!"
The vendors sing from morning to dusk.
Sweet lemonade and fresh-baked treats,
A smile and "Hello" to all we meet! *(smile, wave)*
One last stall with fresh peach pies,
We sing shoo-fly to all those buzzing by. *(shoo pretend bugs)*
With sticky hands and our bags full,
We drive back home and jump in the pool!
Splash!

> **IC2**

More Entries Related to This Topic

Cookout Beanbag Rhyme, p. 88
Firefly, p. 59
Let's Play in the Sand, p. 133
Vacation: A Beanbag Rhyme, p. 165
Watermelon Flannelboard, p. 95

Autumn

188 ***Apple-Dapple**

Use a real or artificial apple as you say this rhyme, and say one verse for each child as the apple is rolled to him or her.

Apple-dapple-ony,
The apple rolls to Tony.
Apple-dapple-isa,
The apple rolls to Lisa . . .

Continue until all the children have received the apple.

> **IC2**

189 **Apple Flannelboard Song** (to the tune of "B-I-N-G-O")

There was a farmer, picked some fruit,
And apple was its name, oh.
A-P-P-L-E,

A-P-P-L-E,
A-P-P-L-E,
And apple was its name, oh.

Repeat, gradually replacing each letter with claps. Each time you replace a letter with a clap, replace the flannelboard letter with an apple.

IC2, IC3

190 ***Pumpkin Feelings Magnetboard Song*** (to the tune of "If You're Happy and You Know It")

Print out several large pumpkins (from the template) and laminate them. Attach magnetic strips to the back and place the pumpkins on the magnetboard. Invite the children to help you decorate your pumpkins. Ask the children to suggest different feelings the pumpkins could show. For each feeling, ask them to describe what the pumpkin would look like if it were showing that feeling. For example, a happy pumpkin would be smiling). Then use a dry-erase marker to draw the pumpkin's face before singing the following song.

If you're a happy pumpkin, show a smile.
If you're a happy pumpkin, show a smile.
If you're a happy pumpkin, then your smile will surely show it.
If you're a happy pumpkin, show a smile.

If you're a sad pumpkin, cry some tears . . .
If you're a scared pumpkin, widen your eyes . . .
If you're a silly pumpkin, stick out your tongue . . .

IC2, IE5, IE6

191 ***Pumpkin Patch Match***

Print out twice as many pumpkin shapes (from the template) as you expect to have children in your storytime. Create different matching pairs of pumpkins by drawing shapes, letters, or numbers on each pair. (For older children, you may wish to use autumn vocabulary words, such as *pumpkin*, *apple*, *fall*, and *squirrel*.) Place one pumpkin from each pair on the board, and pass out the others to the children. Say the following rhyme and help the children find their matches.

Pumpkin, pumpkin, in the patch.
Use your eyes and make a match!
Look at your pumpkin: if it's a _____ you see,
Bring your pumpkin up to me!

IC2, IE5

More Entries Related to This Topic

*Apples Big and Apples Small, p. 87

5 Jack-O-Lanterns Flannelboard, p. 101

5 Little Apples, p. 143

5 Little Pilgrims Flannelboard, p. 102

Popcorn Rhyme, p. 94

The Worm's House, p. 23

Recommended Books

Tap Tap Boom Boom by Elizabeth Bluemle. Somerville, MA: Candlewick, 2014.

Mystery Vine: A Pumpkin Surprise by Cathryn Falwell. New York: Greenwillow, 2009.

Daytime Nighttime by William Low. New York: Henry Holt, 2014.

Tap the Magic Tree by Christie Matheson. New York: Greenwillow, 2013.

Lola Plants a Garden by Anna McQuinn. Watertown, MA: Charlesbridge, 2014.

Sophie's Squash by Pat Zietlow Miller. New York: Schwartz and Wade Books, 2013.

Hands and Hearts by Donna Jo Napoli. New York: Abrams, 2014.

A Kitten Tale by Eric Rohman. New York: Knopf, 2008.

Winter Walk by Virginia Brimhall Snow. Layton, UT: Gibbs Smith, 2014.

Little Owl's Night by Divya Srinivasan. New York: Viking, 2011.

13

People in My Neighborhood

192 Baker, Baker

Before sharing this action rhyme, discuss the steps involved in baking bread. List the steps on a whiteboard, chalkboard, or piece of flipchart paper, and then act out each step as you say the rhyme.

Baker, baker, stir the dough.
Baker, baker, knead it like so.
Baker, baker, let it rise.
Now put it in a pan the right size.

Baker, baker, punch it down.
Baker, baker, let it sit around.
Now into the oven, in the heat, heat, heat.
Take it out, let it cool, then we eat, eat, eat!

IA1, IC2, IE4

193 Doctor, Doctor

Use a toy doctor kit and the following props: a teddy bear, a box of bandages, a pillow and blanket, a medicine cup or spoon. Let the children take turns being the doctor and choosing a remedy for the teddy bear.

Doctor, doctor, help me quick.
I am here 'cause I'm sick, sick, sick!
I fell down and cut my knee!
What can you do to help me? *(apply bandage)*

Doctor, doctor, help me quick.
I am here 'cause I'm sick, sick, sick!
I don't feel good, nothing looks yummy.
Can you give me something to help my tummy? *(pretend to give medicine)*

Doctor, doctor, help me quick.
I am here 'cause I'm sick, sick, sick!
I'm dizzy and tired and achy, too.
Can you tell me what I should do? *(lie down with blanket and pillow)*

> **IC2, IE5**

194 **The Farmer** (to the tune of "The Wheels on the Bus")

The farmer in the field plants the seeds, seeds, seeds,
Seeds, seeds, seeds,
Seeds, seeds, seeds.
The farmer in the field plants seeds, seeds, seeds to feed you and me.

The farmer picks the veggies from the plant,
From the plant,
From the plant.
The farmer picks the veggies from the plant to feed you and me.

We buy the fruit and vegetables from the market,
From the market,
From the market.
We buy the fruit and vegetables from the market and gobble them all up!
Chomp!

> **IC2, IE5**

195 **5 Firefighters**

5 little firefighters fast asleep
When the alarm sounds with a beep beep beep!
1 firefighter slides down the pole,
A second grabs her fire suit, her boots, and hose!
The third firefighter grabs her ax and ladder,
The fourth firefighter says, "I wonder what's the
       matter?"
The fifth firefighter puts her hat on her head,
And they all jump in the truck that is red!

> **IC2, IIA1, IIA4, IIA5**

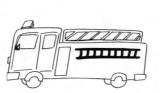

196 Food Helpers

Rub-a-dub-dub, three people in the tub,
And who do you think they be?
The grocer, the baker, and the farmer,
They all help to feed me!

IC2, IE5

197 In My Neighborhood (to the tune of "Good Morning Baltimore" from *Hairspray*)

Good morning, Mom and Dad,
It's sunny and I'm oh so glad,
There's a lot of people to see,
In my community.

There's the barber who cuts my hair,
When he's done all the people stare.
I look like a beauty queen,
A star from the silver screen.

Good morning to the florist,
Her flowers are like a chorus,
An explosion of colors,
Roses outdo all the others!

Hello Mr. Mailman,
Are there letters in your van,
Something special for me to see,
A package or treat for me?

The grocer has the best fresh bread,
To keep us all well fed,
With fresh vegetable soup for dinner,
The day was a winner.

Goodnight, my neighborhood,
The day was oh so good.
I love all the friends I met,
Tomorrow I'll visit the vet!

IC2, IE5

198 So Many Shoes Flannelboard

Place the shoes on one side of the flannelboard and the people on the other. One by one, work with the children to match the shoe to the occupation. As you present each shoe, make sure to use words that describe the shoe and its function. For example, you might say, "This is a boot. It's very sturdy and has a strong steel toe, so if you drop something on your foot it won't hurt you. Who might need a shoe like that?"

IC2, IE5

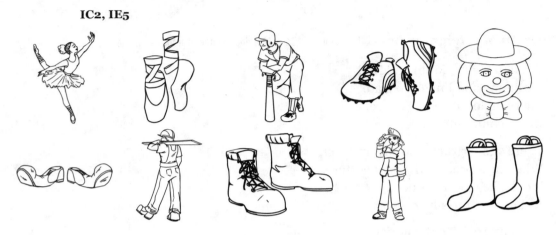

199 Super Song (to the tune of "B-I-N-G-O")

There was a kid who wore a cape,
She was a superhero.
S-U-P-E-R,
S-U-P-E-R,
S-U-P-E-R,
She was a superhero!

Repeat, gradually replacing each letter with Superman-like arm movements or claps.

IC2, IC3

200 Superhero, It's Just a Job

I'm a damsel in distress and a dragon is chasing me,
His fire is very hot, as you can plainly see.
I call for help, "Someone save me!"
And a hero arrives in answer to my plea!
With a *Pow, Wham, Boom,* he saves the day again!
A superhero's job is to conquer the villain!

I'm a little boy who became too greedy,
I climbed the beanstalk, but now the giant's chasing me.
I call for help, "Someone save me!"
And a hero arrives in answer to my plea!
With a *Pow, Wham, Boom,* he saves the day again!
A superhero's job is to conquer the villain!

I'm in the wrong place at the wrong time,
When the robber arrives in the bank, I'm collecting my dimes.
I call for help, "Someone save me!"
And a hero arrives in answer to my plea!
With a *Pow, Wham, Boom*, he saves the day again!
A superhero's job is to conquer the villain!

      IC2, IE5

201 Mailbox Rhyme

Use real envelopes as props for this rhyme.

I went to the mailbox, and what did I see?
5 little letters waiting for me.
1 for my mommy, 1 for my dad,
1 for sister Judy, 1 for brother Brad.
That leaves 1 letter more—
Who could it be for?
I look at the envelope, and then I see:
The last letter in the mailbox is just for me!

      IC2, IE5, IIA1, IIA4, IIA5

202 Restaurant Rhyme

Give each child a scarf to use during the rhyme.

Welcome to my restaurant, open the door and come in. *(hold scarf up flat in front of you and move it as if opening a door)*
Take off your coat and have a seat, and soon your meal will begin. *(use scarf to wave imaginary customer to imaginary seat)*
I'll be your server, and I'll take your order. *(fold scarf over arm as if it is a towel)*
What would you like to eat?
Spaghetti or tacos? Soup or salad? Fish sticks or maybe some meat?
I'll write down what you want on my handy notepad, *(hold scarf as notepad and "write" on it)*
I'll bring you some bread and a drink. *(hold scarf as a pitcher and "pour" drink)*
And then a platter with just what you ordered—it's much more food than you think! *(hold scarf flat out over hands like a tray)*
And when you're all done, wipe your face with your napkin, *(use scarf as napkin)*
Pay your bill and you're off on your way. *(wave scarf to show customer walking out door)*
I'll clean up the table the best I am able, *(use scarf to "wipe" imaginary table)*
To serve my next customer today!

      IC2, IE5

203 *The Tightrope Walker: A Beanbag Rhyme

Place a masking tape line on the floor to act as a tightrope. Invite the children to balance their beanbags on their heads as they walk across. If they drop the beanbags, encourage the children to pick up the bags and keep trying!

With my beanbag on my head,
I stand so very tall.
I walk along my own tightrope
And will not let it fall.

      IC2

204 *Truck Driver, Truck Driver Flannelboard

This activity would be an excellent follow-up to *Truck Driver Tom* by Monica Wellington (New York: Dutton, 2007).

Make multiples of the items to go in the truck, enough for every child to get a piece. Pass the pieces out before you say the rhyme. When you announce what the truck is carrying, have the children with those items come up and place the pieces on the board.

Truck Driver, Truck Driver, what do you say?
What are you carrying in your truck today?
I am carrying apples!

Repeat with other items.

      IC2, IE5

205 Where Do I Go?

I need to send a letter to my friend at camp,
Where can I go to buy a stamp?
Where do I go? *(post office)*

I need to buy donuts to surprise my dad,
I know he will be really glad!
Where do I go? *(bakery)*

I don't have money to buy a book,
Where can I borrow one and take a look?
Where do I go? *(library)*

My grandma gave me a nickel to save,
Where can I take it for a rainy day?
Where do I go? *(bank)*

My brother has a fever and feels real sick,
He needs something to make him feel better quick!
Where do I go? *(doctor)*

Mom says I've been good and she'll take me to lunch,
I can eat my favorite food with a munch, munch, munch.
Where do I go? *(restaurant)*

IC2, IE5

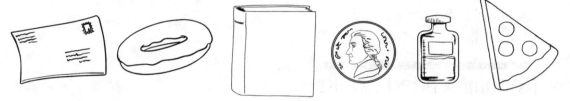

206 Who Do We Call?

Place the pieces on the board and encourage the children to guess which one each clue refers to.

Emergency, emergency, who do we call?
A cat's stuck in the tree and I don't want him to fall.
We need to call a . . . (firefighter!)

Emergency, emergency, who do we call?
A burglar tried to break into a store at the mall!
We need to call a . . . (police officer!)

Emergency, emergency, who do we call?
My puppy is very sick, he tried to eat the baseball.
We need to call a . . . (veterinarian!)

Emergency, emergency, who do we call?
Humpty Dumpty fell off the very tall wall.
We need to call a . . . (doctor!)

IC2, IE5

More Entries Related to This Topic

Recommended Books

* *The Sounds Around Town* by Maria Carluccio. Cambridge, MA: Barefoot Books, 2008.

Night Shift by Jessie Hartland. New York: Bloomsbury, 2007.

Police: Hurrying! Helping! Saving! by Patricia Hubbell. Tarrytown, NY: Marshall Cavendish, 2008.

Teacher! Sharing, Helping, Caring by Patricia Hubbell. Tarrytown, NY: Marshall Cavendish, 2009.

Say Hello! by Rachel Isadora. New York: Putnam, 2010.

Albert the Fix-It Man by Janet Lord. Atlanta, GA: Peachtree, 2008.

Squeak! Rumble! Whomp! Whomp! Whomp! A Sonic Adventure by Wynton Marsalis. Somerville, MA: Candlewick, 2012.

Bug Patrol by Denise Dowling Mortensen. New York: Clarion, 2013.

Percy's Neighborhood by Stuart J. Murphy. Watertown, MA: Charlesbridge, 2013.

Whose Shoes? A Shoe for Every Job by Stephen R. Swinburne. Honesdale, PA: Boyds Mills Press, 2010.

14
Play

207 ***Ball Balance Song** (to the tune of "Here We Go 'Round the Mulberry Bush")

The ball is balanced on my hand,
On my hand, on my hand.
The ball is balanced on my hand,
Until I make it bounce.

The ball is balanced on my foot . . .
The ball is balanced on my head . . .

      IC2, IE5

208 **Bouncy Ball**

Invite the children to bounce an imaginary ball as you say this rhyme.

Bouncy ball, bouncy ball,
Where will you go?
Bounce it to the corner
When you throw!

Bouncy ball, bouncy ball,
Where will you go?

Bounce it up and down,
On your toe.

Bouncy ball, bouncy ball,
Where will you go?
Bounce it on your head,
While shaking it "no."

Bouncy ball, bouncy ball,
Where will you go?
Sit it in your lap,
Nice and slow.

IC2, IE5

209 *5 Little Balls Flannelboard (to the tune of "5 Little Ducks")

5 little balls rolled out to play
At the playground one sunny day.
Teacher called them in with a *clap, clap, clap*.
4 little balls came rolling back.

4 little balls . . .
3 little balls . . .
2 little balls . . .
1 little ball . . .
Teacher called them in with a *clap, clap, clap*.
5 little balls came rolling back!

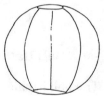

You could also act out this song with real balls and have the children
roll them back to you each time.

IC2, IE5, IIA1, IIA4, IIA5, IIB1

210 5 Little Friends Jumping on the Bed

5 little friends jumping on the bed,
Bumped their heads like Mama said!
1 little friend was so sad,
She/He went home and then we had . . .

4 little friends . . .
3 little friends . . .
2 little friends . . .

1 little friend jumping on the bed,
Bumped his head like Mama said!
1 little friend was so sad,
Mama held him tight and he was glad.

IC2, IE5, IIA1, IIA4, IIA5, IIB1

211 5 Little Kites

1 little kite in a sky so blue,
Along came another and then there were 2.
2 little kites flying above the trees,
Along came another and then there were 3.
3 little kites soaring past the door,
Along came another and then there were 4.
4 little kites pass a beehive,
Along came another and then there were 5.
5 little kites on a windy day,
Along came a big wind and blew them away!

IC2, IE5, IIA1, IIA4, IIA5

212 Hula Hoop

Mime using a hula hoop throughout this rhyme. During the last line, bend your knees as if the hula hoop is getting lower, and end by sitting on the ground.

Hula hoop, hula hoop, to and fro.
Hula hoop, hula hoop, here we go.
Hula hoop, hula hoop, 'round your tummy.
Hula hoop, hula hoop, feels so funny.
Hula hoop, hula hoop, 'round and 'round.
Hula hoop, hula hoop, down . . . to . . . the . . . ground.

IC2, IE5

213 Let's Play in the Sand (to the tune of "Let's Go Fly a Kite")

With sunshine and a beach day,
You can be sure that you will play.
With your shovel and pail,
And a blow-up toy whale,
You're ready to start,
Creating some sand art!

Oh, oh, oh!
Let's play in the sand,
The day will be grand,
Let's get our toys and build a castle.
Hurry, build a moat,
And get a toy boat,
Oh, let's build a sand castle.

IC2, IE5

214 Nesting Dolls

Move the smaller dolls behind the larger one as they "nest," and uncover them as they pop back out.

Little doll, little doll, have a rest,
Hop inside to where you nest.
Medium doll, medium doll, have a rest,
Hop inside to where you nest.
Big doll, big doll, on her own,
Swaying and wishing she wasn't alone.
How I wish I had a friend,
Pop—medium doll is here again!
Are there any more friends today?
Pop—little doll is here to stay!

IC2, IE5, IIA2

215 Playground Romp

As you say each verse of the rhyme, sign the sign that goes with it.

At the playground, *(sign PLAYGROUND)*
Always so much fun.
Watching all the kids
On the run.

Twisty slide, twisty slide, *(sign SLIDE)*
Climbing to the top.
Slide all the way down
With a great big *Plop.*

On the seesaw, *(sign SEESAW)*
Going back and forth.
We go so fast
We get dizzy of course.

Flying on the swing set, *(sign SWING)*
We go so high!
We say hello
To all the birds flying by!

IC2, IE5

playground

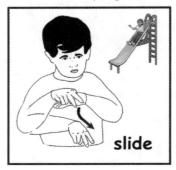

slide

seesaw

swing

216 Rubber Ducky

I am a rubber ducky and I say quack, quack, quack,
If you put me in your bathtub I'll squirt water on your back.
I'm yellow and I squeak, that's what rubber duckies do,
I'll be your best water friend because I love you! *(give yourself a hug)*

IC2, IE5

217 *Seesaw: A Partner Rhyme

Each child faces a partner, holding hands. On the word *seesaw*, they alternate up and down movements as if they are on a seesaw.

Seesaw, seesaw, up and down.
Seesaw, seesaw, turn around. *(hold hands and turn in a circle)*
Seesaw, seesaw, to and fro.
Seesaw, seesaw, here we go! *(speed up the seesaw and repeat the rhyme)*

IC2, IE5

218 *The Seesaw Flannelboard

Based on the book by Judith Koppens (New York: Clavis, 2013)

Giraffe's friends are too light to play on the seesaw with him, until they work together so they can all play.

IA1, IA2, IA3, IID2

219 *Small Bunny's Blue Blanket Scarf Story

Based on the book by Tatyana Feeney (New York: Random House, 2012)

Small Bunny loves his blue blanket, and he thinks it's perfect just the way it is. His mother does not agree, and when she insists on washing it, a great deal of swinging, painting, reading, and playing with the blanket are required before it feels right again.

Pass out scarves or pieces of fabric for the children to use as you tell the story. Invite the children to move their blankets in the following ways:

swinging: sway scarves back and forth

painting: bunch up scarf and use it as a brush

reading: snuggle the scarf

hiding: put the scarf behind your back

washing and drying blanket: swirl scarf around

hanging up blanket: pretend to hang scarf

hugging: wrap scarf around you

IA1, IA2, IA3

220   Telephone Rhyme

Use two inactive phones or phone stand-ins made from cardboard for this rhyme. To introduce this rhyme, ask the children how we answer the phone. What are the polite words to say when you answer the phone? Encourage the children to use those words when they have a turn to answer the phone later in the activity.

I'm going to make a telephone call.
I know the phone number, I dial it all.
Ring-a-ling goes the phone, you know what to do.
Answer the phone, 'cause it's for *you!*

Hand the phone to a child and conduct a brief conversation—for example, "Hi, Sadie! How are you? Having fun at storytime? Ready to shake your sillies out soon? Great! Well, I have to go now, got a lot of phone calls to make! Bye!" Repeat the rhyme until all the children have had a turn to answer the phone.

IC2, IE1, IE6

221   What Type of Ball Am I? Flannelboard

Say the rhyme and encourage the children to name the ball from the clues, then place each ball on the flannelboard.

I am an orange ball and I bounce down the court,
I am some people's favorite sport!
What type of ball am I? *(basketball)*

I am a small ball that's hit with a bat,
Sometimes signals are sent when the players touch their hats!
What type of ball am I? *(baseball)*

I am a brown ball tossed by a quarterback,
You need to be careful so he doesn't get sacked.
What type of ball am I? *(football)*

I am a yellow ball that gets hit over a net,
Sometimes a puppy eats me and has to visit the vet.
What type of ball am I? *(tennis)*

I am a black-and-white ball that is kicked in a goal,
If the team wins we'll be on a roll!
What type of ball am I? *(soccer)*

IC2, IE5

222 Yo-Yo Song (to the tune of "I'm a Little Teapot")

Encourage the children to move up and down with you in a rhythmic pattern as you sing the song.

I'm a little yo-yo,
Small and round.
I'm always moving up,
And then back down.
If you keep me going,
We can play,
Up and down we'll go all day!

     IC2, IE5

More Entries Related to This Topic

Recommended Books

Little Sweet Potato by Amy Beth Bloom. New York: HarperCollins, 2012.

Bug and Bear by Ann Bonwill. Tarrytown, NY: Marshall Cavendish, 2011.

Hands Off My Honey! by Jane Chapman. Wilton, CT: Tiger Tales, 2013.

Pirate, Viking and Scientist by Jared Chapman. New York: Little, Brown, 2014.

*Not a Stick by Antoinette Portis. New York: HarperCollins, 2008.

Don't Play with Your Food by Bob Shea. New York: Disney/Hyperion Books, 2014.

Peg Leg Peke by Brie Spangler. New York: Knopf, 2008.

The Tree House That Jack Built by Bonnie Verburg. New York: Orchard Books, 2014.

*Max and Ruby's Treasure Hunt by Rosemary Wells. New York: Penguin, 2012.

*Found by Salina Yoon. New York: Walker, 2014.

15
School and Library

· ·

223 Mary's Animal Mischief

Mary went to school this morning,
As usual, without warning.
But the animals missed her so,
Off to school they too would go.
The lamb showed up, before noon,
Followed by the local raccoon.
When lunch was called, Mary would find
Her chicken was not far behind.
Soon there was an urgent moo,
As Mary's cow appeared out of the blue.
A duck, a rooster, and a cat,
Walked into school and quietly sat.
Suddenly there was a "Neigh,"
Announcing the horse was here to stay.
But when the mouse squeaked "Hello,"
The teacher jumped up and said *"Oh, no!"*
The animals scattered one by one,
Now that they had their fun.

    IC2, IE5

224 Bookmobile (to the tune of "The Wheels on the Bus")

The wheels on the bookmobile go 'round and 'round,
'Round and 'round, 'round and 'round.
The wheels on the bookmobile go 'round and 'round,
Early every morning.

The driver on the bookmobile says, "Check us out,"
"Check us out," "Check us out."
The driver on the bookmobile says, "Check us out,"
Early every morning.

The kids on the bookmobile say, "Let's read this,"
"Let's read this," "Let's read this."
The kids on the bookmobile say, "Let's read this,"
Early every morning.

The parents on the bookmobile say, "Here's our card,"
"Here's our card," "Here's our card."
The parents on the bookmobile say, "Here's our card,"
Early every morning.

The horn on the bookmobile goes honk, honk, honk,
Honk, honk, honk, honk, honk, honk.
The horn on the bookmobile goes honk, honk, honk,
Early every morning.

IC2, IE5

225 *Bunny School: A Learning Fun-for-All* Signing Story

Based on the book by Rick Walton (New York: HarperCollins, 2005)

Bunnies take a rhyming trip through the school day, from making music to sharing during show-and-tell.

As you read or tell the story, teach the school-related signs.

IA1, IA2, IA3, IC2, IE5

school

show

tell

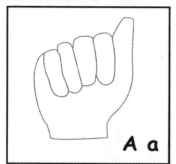

A a

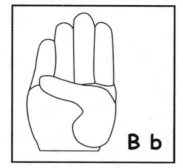

B b

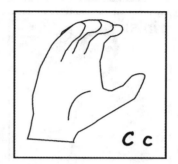

C c

one

two

three

music

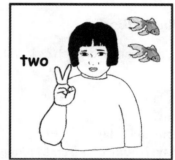

play

eat

science

trip

fire fighter

226 *Children, Children Flannelboard

Make enough child shapes in multiple colors for each child to have one. Pass them out before you say the rhyme.

Children, children, come and play.
It's time to learn at school today.
Red children, *red* children, come and play.
It's time to learn at school today. *(invite children to place red shapes on the flannelboard)*

Repeat with other colors.

All the children are at school today.
Now it's time to learn and play!

Finish by inviting the children to count the shapes of each color and identify which colors have the most shapes on the board and which have the fewest.

IC2, IE5, IIA1, IIA4, IIA5, IID3

227 *Elephant's Story* Flannelboard

Based on the book by Tracey Campbell Pearson (New York: Farrar, Straus and Giroux, 2013)

An elephant accidentally sucks up all the words in a little girl's book and struggles to get them back on the page.

Use a set of magnetic letters along with the flannelboard pieces to help you tell the story.

IA1, IA2, IA3, IC2

228 5 Little Apples

5 little apples on my teacher's desk,
5 shining apples from my class.
1 apple fell off and hit the floor,
Then there were only 4.

4 little apples on my teacher's desk,
4 shining apples from my class.
1 apple made a perfect bed for a bee,
Then there were only 3.

3 little apples on my teacher's desk,
3 shining apples from my class.
1 apple rolled into the glue,
Then there were only 2.

2 little apples on my teacher's desk,
2 shining apples from my class.
1 apple hit the trash and spun,
Then there was only 1.

1 little apple on my teacher's desk,
1 little apple from my class.
My teacher took a big bite from one,
Then *chomp chomp chomp* it was done!

IC2, IE5, IIA1, IIA4, IIA5, IIB1

229 5 Little Books

5 little books at the library,
Waiting for someone to take them to read.
1 little girl chooses a dragon book,
And checks it out to take a look.

4 little books . . . 1 little boy chooses a truck book . . .
3 little books . . . 1 little boy chooses a bear book . . .
2 little books . . . 1 little girl chooses a ballet book . . .
1 little book . . . 1 little girl takes the chicken book . . .

IC2, IE5, IIA1, IIA4, IIA5, IIB1

230 I Like School (to the tune of "Head, Shoulders, Knees, and Toes")

I like school, yes I do, yes I do.
I like school, yes I do, yes I do.
My teacher,
My friends,
And recess too,
I like school, yes I do, yes I do!

IC2

231 Jungle Books Flannelboard

I went to the jungle to see what I could see,
And of course I brought my favorite book with me.
But just when I'd found the perfect reading nook,
The lion said, "Roar," and I dropped my book!
Run away!

I went to the jungle to see what I could see,
And of course I brought my favorite book with me.
But just when I'd found the perfect reading nook,
The monkey said, "Eeee, eeee" and
The lion said, "Roar," and I dropped my book!
Run away!

. . . the snake said, "Hiss" . . .
. . . the elephant said, "Toot" . . .
. . . the hyena said, "Ha" . . .

I went to the jungle to see what I could see,
And of course I brought my favorite book with me.
But just when I'd found the perfect reading nook,
The animals all came around, so I read them my book!

IA1, IA2, IA3, IC2, IE5

232 Library Books

There's magic at the library when I check out a book,
I open the pages and take a look.
Sometimes I see a dragon in a cave
And read about knights who are so brave.
Other times I travel on a boat,
Or see great armies who cross the moat.
There are books about Halloween full of bats,
And some are full of scary cats.
Other books are full of girls that dance,
But I like books that show when the reindeer prance!

IC2, IE5

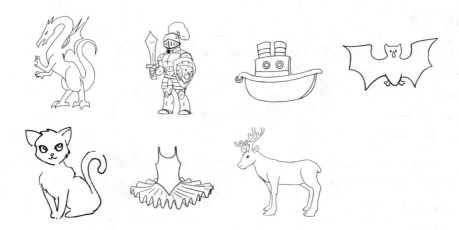

233 My Teacher

My teacher is nice,
Her smile is wide.
She gives us little treats,
And is happy when we try.
She helps us with our letters,
And our numbers too,
And if we stumble,
She helps us tie our shoes.

IC2

234 *Ollie's School Day: A Yes-and-No Book* Signing Story

Based on the book by Stephanie Calmenson (New York: Holiday House, 2012)

Readers are invited to answer a series of silly yes and no questions as Ollie gets ready for school and makes his way through the school day.

Teach the children the ASL signs YES and NO and invite them to answer with their signs as you read the questions.

IA1, IA2, IA3, IC2, IE5

235 Shelving Game

Preparation: Cover five books with brown paper and write the following titles and authors on each:

Ants by Adam Adams   *Dogs* by Dana Dawson

Bears by Byron Best   *Elephants* by Edna Edwards

Cats by Carrie Carter

Underline the first letter of the author's last name on each cover and write that letter on the spine. Post an alphabet line in your storytime room to help with the activity.

Hello, friends, come with me,
Help me sort my library!
We've got to put the books in a row,

In the proper order just so.
We need to remember our ABCs.
Come and shelve the storybooks with me!

Hold up one of the books and read the title and author's name, pointing out each. Explain that storybooks are kept in order by the author's last name, so that readers can find all the storybooks by that author in one place. Ask the children to identify the first letter of the author's last name and point it out on the spine, too. Place the book spine-out on a small shelf or cart, then repeat the process for the next book. Ask the children whether the next book goes before or after the one already on the shelf. Refer to the alphabet line for help and sing the beginning of the alphabet song, too. Repeat until you have put all the books in order.

IC1, IC2, IE5

236 Teacher Song (to the tune of "The Wheels on the Bus")

My teacher greets the class and says, "Please sit down,"
"Please sit down," "Please sit down."
My teacher greets the class and says, "Please sit down," each and every day.

My teacher helps us learn our ABCs . . .
My teacher helps us practice handwriting . . .
My teacher helps us learn our 1-2-3s . . .

IC2, IE5

237 What's in My Backpack?

Place the items on the board and ask the children to point to the one being described in each line.

What's in my backpack on this first day of school?
I'll definitely need a writing tool! *(pencil)*
If I want to draw a picture for my mother,
I'll need something with different colors. *(crayons)*
When I need to cut in a straight line,
These will do the job just fine. *(scissors)*
The paper flowers need to stick on a background of blue,
What item do I need to choose? *(glue)*
I've worked all morning and my tummy rumbles,
If I don't eat soon, I'll surely grumble! *(lunch)*

IC2, IE5

More Entries Related to This Topic

A Balloon's Tale: A Prop Story, p. 11

Can You Draw a Shape?, p. 68

*5 Little Balls Flannelboard, p. 132

Liking Song, p. 14

A la rueda, rueda / 'Round, 'Round the Ring: A Circle Rhyme from Venezuela, p. 42

Recommended Books

How to Bake a Book by Ella Burfoot. Naperville, IL: Sourcebooks, 2014.

Foxy by Emma Dodd. New York: Scholastic, 2012.

Check It Out! Reading, Finding, Helping by Patricia Hubbell. Tarrytown, NY: Marshall Cavendish, 2011.

Mary and Her Little Lamb: The True Story of the Famous Nursery Rhyme by Will Moses. New York: Philomel, 2011.

Hickory Dickory Dog by Alison Murray. Somerville, MA: Candlewick, 2014.

The Best Day in Room A: Sign Language for School Activities by Dawn Babb Prochovnic. Edina, MN: Magic Wagon, 2010.

Dinosaur vs. School by Bob Shea. New York: Hyperion, 2014.

Dinosaur vs. the Library by Bob Shea. New York: Hyperion, 2011.

Red Knit Cap Girl and the Reading Tree by Naoko Stoop. New York: Little, Brown, 2014.

Seven Little Mice Go to School by Haruo Yamashita. New York: NorthSouth Books, 2011.

16

Sing and Dance

· ·

Movement and Dance

238 Circle Song (to the tune of "The Farmer in the Dell")

Invite the children to move around the circle in different ways as you sing the song.

A-walking we will go,
A-walking we will go,
Hi-ho, the derry-o,
A-walking we will go.

A-skipping we will go . . .
A-hopping we will go . . .
A-dancing we will go . . .
A-tiptoe we will go . . .

     IC2, IE5

239 **Color Dance** (to the tune of "Dance, Dance, Dance" by the Beach Boys)

Place large dots on the floor in red, blue, and yellow and have the children step on them as you sing the song.

After sleeping all night, I am ready to dance,
I push the radio on and turn it up all the way.
I gotta dance (dance, dance, dance on the red dot) right on the dot,
(Dance, dance, dance on the blue dot),
The beat's really hot.
(Dance, dance, dance on the yellow dot),
Dance (dance) dance (dance) dance (dance) yeah!
When I feel really angry I try to shake it off quick,
With my mom by my side the music does the trick.
I gotta dance (dance, dance, dance on the red dot) right on the dot,
(Dance, dance, dance on the blue dot),
The beat's really hot.
(Dance, dance, dance on the yellow dot),
Dance (dance) dance (dance) dance (dance) yeah!

      IC2, IE5

240 *Dancing Feet!* **Flannelboard**

Based on the book by Lindsey Craig (New York: Knopf, 2010)

A variety of animals, from tiptoeing ladybugs to stomping elephants, show off their dance moves in this vibrant, easy-to-read picture book.

Make a path of life-size footprints around the storytime room, ten for each animal. As you read the story, first show the page that invites the children to guess the animal, followed by the page identifying the animal. Invite the children to move along the path in that animal's footprints, moving like that animal, before going on to the next page. If you prefer, or for a larger group, use large magnetboard pieces to identify the animals instead, and ask the children to identify the animal based on the words and the animal's footprints on the path.

      IA1, IA2, IA3, IC2, IE5

241 **Happy Dance**

Whistle a tune,
Do-si-do,
Dance around,
On your toes.

Bow to your partner,
Wave to the right,
Dance in a circle,
Hold yourself tight.

Raise your arms high,
Sway in the breeze,
Swoop down low,
And bend your knees.

IC2, IE5

242 *Little Jumping Joan (adapted traditional)

Here I am, little jumping Joan.
When nobody's with me, I'm always alone.

. . . little clapping Joan . . .
. . . little stomping Joan . . .
. . . little spinning Joan . . .

Here I am, little dancing Joan.
When my friends are with me, I'm not alone!

IC2, IE5

243 **Rhymin' Simon**

Use a puppet or stuffed animal to play Simon.

My friend Simon loves to rhyme!
He loves to play this game all the time.
He'll say one word that's something to do,
And then another word, and that makes two.
If the two words rhyme, do what the first word says.
But if they don't, say "No rhyme!" instead.
Simon says: jump, bump. (Jump *and* bump *rhyme! Let's jump!*)
Simon says: sing, ring. (Sing *and* ring *rhyme! Let's sing! La la la!*)
Simon says: spin, pan. *(No rhyme!)*
Simon says: spin, pin. (Spin *and* pin *rhyme! Let's spin!*)

Repeat with more word pairs:

Walk, lake

Walk, talk

Hop, pop

Clap, cake

Clap, strap

Wiggle, jiggle

Wave, white

Wave, pave

IC2, IE5

244 *Shake Your Eggs

Eggs for breakfast, eggs for lunch,
Eggs for dinner, I have a hunch
You can do what I can do:
Shake your egg in front of you!

Eggs for breakfast, eggs for lunch,
Eggs for dinner, I have a hunch
You will do the thing I beg:
Shake your egg down by your leg!

. . . You can give this thing a try:
Shake your egg way up high!

. . . You can try this thing I found:
Shake your egg around and around!

. . . You can shake your egg just so:
Shake your egg high and low!

IC2, IE5

245 Swing Step

Twirl to the left,
And twirl to the right.
Give yourself a big hug,
And squeeze yourself tight.

Step to the left,
And step to the right.
Smile to the crowds,
Cheering with all their might.

Clap to the left,
And clap to the right.
Hold up your hands,
And fly a kite!

Wave to the left,
And wave to the right.
Say good-bye to your friends,
In the dwindling light.

IC2, IE5

More Entries Related to This Topic

Bear Is Sad: A Participation Story, p. 12

*Fairy Dance, p. 72

Windy Moves, p. 84

*A Zoo on Our Heads, p. 28

Music

246 **The Beat of the Music Flannelboard**

Swaying to the music,
Hear the beat of the drum,
Rat-tat-tat,
Hum, hum, hum.

Swaying to the music,
Listen to the trumpet roar,
The notes go higher,
Soar, soar, soar.

Swaying to the music,
The saxophone sings the blues,
The sound going lower,
Woo, woo, woo.

Swaying to the music,
The piano finishes the tale,
Fingers dancing over the keys,
Sail, sail, sail.

IC2, IE5

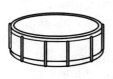   

247 I Went to the Concert Flannelboard and Sound Story

Find links to free downloadable sound files to use with this story at www.storytimestuff.net.

I went to the concert and what did I hear? *(play a sound and have the children guess what it is)*

The sound of a piano in my ear! *(show the flannelboard piece)*

Repeat with other instruments.

> **IC2, IE5**

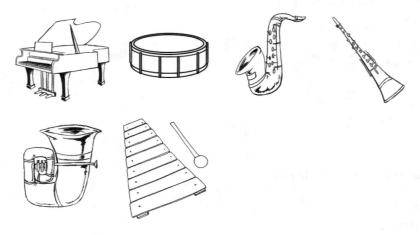

248 Musical Me

I can play my violin with a zin, zin, zin. *(mime playing violin)*
I can play my flute with a toot, toot, toot. *(mime playing flute)*
I can play my saxophone with a moan, moan, moan. *(mime playing saxophone)*
I can play my drum with a pum, pum, pum. *(mime playing drum)*
But even with no instruments,
The music's still in me.
I can clap my hands *(clap hands)*
And stamp my feet *(stamp feet)*
And sing la-da-dee-dee! *(sing dramatically)*

> **IC2, IE5**

249 The Zoo Symphony: An Action Story

The animals were so excited. The Symphony Orchestra was performing at the zoo! The animals listened to the beautiful music. *(play classical music)*
Then they noticed the instruments. What instruments do you hear? *(encourage children to identify the instruments they hear and take time to mime playing them; show pictures of different kinds of instruments)*
Then they noticed the lady standing at the front of the orchestra, waving a special stick called a baton. What was she doing? *(take answers from the children)*
That lady was the conductor, and she was helping all the musicians to stay together and make sure all the music was following the same beat. Let's all pretend that

we are holding batons like a conductor. Can you move your baton to the beat? Let's count: 1-2-3-4, 1-2-3-4.

Well, the animals got pretty excited about this. They all wanted to conduct the orchestra! The conductor decided to let them try. First the elephant conducted with her trunk! Can you be an elephant conductor? *(encourage kids to make trunks with arms and conduct for a bit)*

Then the monkey said, "My turn! I will use my tail!" *(make monkey tails with arms and conduct)*

Then the octopus said, "I will conduct with my tentacles!" *(pretend arms are tentacles and conduct)*

Then the snake said, "I don't have any arms or legs. I will use my tongue!" *(conduct with tongue)*

Can you think of other animals that would like to conduct? *(let the children come up with different ideas and take the time to act out each one)*

Then the conductor said, "It's time for the big finish!" *(conduct in sweeping gestures)*

"Thank you to all of our guest conductors today here at the zoo!"

IC2, IE5, IIA1

Transitional Activities

250 *Jumping

Jumping 1 and jumping 2,
Touch the floor, then touch your shoe.
Jumping 3 and jumping 4,
Turn around and jump some more.
Jumping 5 and jumping 6,
Play a rhythm with pretend drumsticks.
Jumping 7 and jumping 8,
Push real hard and shut the gate.
Jumping 9 and jumping 10,
Then settle into your place again.

IC2, IE5, IIA1

251 Up and Down Rhyme

Each time you say "Up, down" in the following rhyme, raise and lower your hands.

Up, down, up, down,
Dance, dance, dance.
Up, down, up, down,
Prance, prance, prance.
Up, down, up, down,
Jump, jump, jump.
Up, down, up, down,

Sit with a bump.
Up, down, up, down,
Clap, clap, clap.
Up, down, up, down,
Hands in your lap!

      IC2, IE5

252 **Up and Down Song** (to the tune of "My Bonnie Lies Over the Ocean")

I like to turn 'round in a circle.
I like to bounce all around.
I like to stamp my feet.
I like to reach up and then down.
Up, down,
Up, down,
Then wiggle my arms all around, around.
Up, down,
Up, down,
Then sit my bottom right down.

      IC2, IE5

253 **The Way to Londontown** (adapted traditional)

Seesaw, sacaradown,
Which is the way to Londontown?
One foot up, the other foot down,
That is the way to Londontown.
Seesaw, sacaradown,
Which is the way to Londontown?
Two arms up, two arms down,
That is the way to Londontown.
Seesaw, sacaradown,
Which is the way to Londontown?
Clap your hands and turn around,
That is the way to Londontown.
Seesaw, sacaradown,
Which is the way to Londontown?
Jump up high, then sit right down.
That is the way to Londontown.

      IC2, IE5

More Entries Related to This Topic

Recommended Books

Firebird by Misty Copeland. New York: Putnam, 2014.

Chirchir Is Singing by Kelly Cunnane. New York: Schwartz and Wade Books, 2011.

Rupert Can Dance by Jules Feiffer. New York: Farrar, Straus and Giroux, 2014.

Wiggle Giggle Tickle Train by Nora Hilb and Sharon Jennings. Toronto, ON: Annick Press, 2009.

Little Diva by LaChanze. New York: Feiwel and Friends, 2010.

Can You Dance to the Boogaloo? by Alice V. Lickens. London: Pavilion, 2013.

Pete the Cat and His Four Groovy Buttons by Eric Litwin. New York: HarperCollins, 2012.

Let's Dance, Grandma! by Nigel McMullen. New York: HarperCollins, 2014.

I Got the Rhythm by Connie Schofield-Morrison. New York: Bloomsbury, 2014.

Frances Dean Who Loved to Dance and Dance by Birgitta Sif. Somerville, MA: Candlewick, 2014.

17 Transportation

254 *Airplane, Airplane

Airplane, airplane, take off slow.
Spread your wings and up you go!
Airplane, airplane in the sky
Airplane, airplane, zooming high!

IC2, IE5

255 Bears on the Bus Flannelboard

Prepare ten to twenty bear shapes for this activity.

Once upon a time there was a bus. Early in the morning, the bus driver started it up
and went to his first stop. Two little bears got on the bus. Let's count them: 1, 2.
Then the driver went to the next stop. Two more bears got on. Now how many bears
are on the bus? 1, 2, 3, 4: 2 bears plus 2 bears equals 4 bears!
The bus driver went on to the next stop, and there one of the bears got off—he was
going to visit his grandmother. Now how many bears are on the bus? Let's
count! 1, 2, 3.

Continue with more stops, adding and removing bears as desired to create different counting
challenges. When you are ready to wind down the story, start having the bears get off the bus
and ask the children to suggest destinations for them.

Now there were no bears on the bus. It was time for the driver to go home and have dinner. Bye-bye, bus!

IC2, IE5, IE6, IIA1, IIA4, IIA5, IIB1, IIB2

256 The Bridge to Old Dundeedle

There once was a bridge,
A very strong bridge *(lace fingers together to form a "bridge" between the hands)*
'Twas the bridge to old Dundeedle.
But the people marched over with a tramp tramp tramp *(bounce bridge as if people are marching across)*
And the wood fell prey to the cold and the damp
And down fell some pieces with a hamp, kamp, gamp, *(drop thumbs)*
Off the bridge to old Dundeedle.

Repeat four more times, dropping the index fingers, middle fingers, ring fingers, and then pinky fingers so that the bridge gets thinner each time and is eventually gone. Make your voice smaller each time to show the diminishing size of the bridge.

"Oh, where is our bridge, our very strong bridge?" *(hold fists up to show that the bridge is gone)*
Cried the people of old Dundeedle.
So they dragged and they stacked *(slowly extend and interlock fingers over the next three lines)*
And they sawed and they hacked
And they worked together till the bridge was back,
The bridge to old Dundeedle! *(strongly interlock fingers to show completed bridge)*

IC2, IE5

257 Chugga-chugga

Move arms in a circular motion and step forward and backward to imitate the motion of a train as you say this rhyme.

Chugga-chugga, chugga-chugga
Train comes down the track.
It's always moving forward,
Never moving back.
Chugga-chugga, chugga-chugga
See how fast it goes.

People cover up their ears
When the whistle blows!
Tooooooooot!

IC2, IE5

258 **Color Train Magnetboard Story and Song** (to the tune of "The Farmer in the Dell")

Make nine boxcars in red, orange, yellow, green, blue, purple, black, brown, and white as well as enough items so that every child gets one. It's okay to have multiples of some items.

Once there was a special train that carried many different items. But this train had special boxcars, and everything in the train was sorted by color! The conductor would sing a special song while he loaded the items into the train. First, he would start by putting all the red items into the red boxcar. He would sing this song:

Oh, everything that's red,
Everything that's red
Will go into the red boxcar.
Yes, everything that's red. *(invite children with red items to place them in the red boxcar, then review each item)*

Repeat with orange, yellow, green, blue, purple, black, brown, and white items.

IC2, IE5, IID3

259 5 Boats Flannelboard

5 little boats floating in the sea,
5 little boats sailing past me.
Along comes the wind with a great big gust,
And 1 little boat is lost to us.

4 little boats . . .
3 little boats . . .
2 little boats . . .

1 little boat floating in the sea,
1 little boat sailing past me.
The wind is tired, it's barely a breeze,
So 1 little boat can float with ease!

IC2, IE5, IIA1, IIA4, IIA5, IIB1

260 *Going on a Trip Magnetboard Song

(to the tune of "Bumpin' Up and Down in My Little Red Wagon")

Place all the pieces in a bag. Let the children take turns pulling items from the bag to determine which verse you will sing next. Invite the children to act out each means of communication as you walk, drive, pretend to bike, and so on in a circle.

Goin' on a trip, going to the city,
Goin' on a trip, going to the city,
Goin' on a trip, going to the city,
How will we get there?

Driving in the car with a vroom, vroom, vroom, vroom . . .
Riding on the train with a woo, woo, woo, woo . . .
Flying in a plane with a zoom, zoom, zoom, zoom . . .
Walking down the street with a right foot, left foot . . .
Rowing in a boat with a row, row, row, row . . .
Biking down the street with a pedal, pedal, pedal, pedal . . .
Riding on the bus with a bump, bump, bump, bump . . .

IC2, IE5

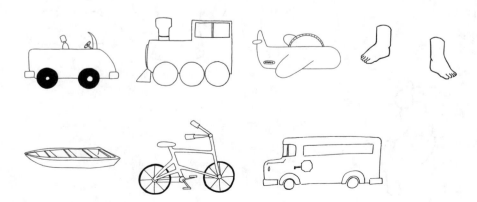

261 Headlights

Headlights, headlights on my car.
Driving near and driving far.
I turn my headlights on and see
All the things in front of me!

IC2, IE5

262 How Will We Get There?

Say each verse and ask the children to guess the means of transportation it describes. Once they have guessed, show the item and place it on the board.

We're going on a trip, we're going far away,
How will we get there, that's the game we'll play!

Rumbling down the runway, lifting in the air,
We're flying in the sky without a care!
How will we get there? *(airplane)*

Bumping up and down, sitting in the cab,
Big wheels turn, this is rad!
How will we get there? *(truck)*

Two wheels, a basket, and pedals too,
Ring, ring, here I come, let me through!
How will we get there? *(bicycle)*

Glub, glub, I'm going under the ocean,
Ping, ping, I move in slow motion.
How will we get there? *(submarine)*

Zip, zoom, this is fun,
Honk, honk, here I come!
How will we get there? *(car)*

IC2, IE5

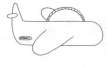 

263 Riding My Bike (to the tune of "The Farmer in the Dell")

Act out the motions as you sing the song.

I'm putting on my helmet,
I'm putting on my helmet,
I'm going to ride my bicycle, so
I'm putting on my helmet.

I'm climbing on my bike . . .
I'm pedaling my bike . . .
I'm looking left and right . . .
I'm slowing down my bike . . .

My bike comes to a stop,
My bike comes to a stop,
I'm done riding my bicycle, so
My bike comes to a stop.

   IC2, IE5

264 Transportation Song (to the tune of "Frère Jacques)

Transportation, transportation.
Here to there, here to there.
Cars and trucks and trains,
Bikes and boats and planes,
Off we go, off we go!

   IC2, IE5

265 Transportation Sounds Game

Say each verse and ask the children to guess the means of transportation it describes. Once they have guessed, show the item and place it on the board.

From afar, then from near,
Vehicles are coming, what do I hear?

Chugga, chugga, chugga, choo, choooooo!
What do I hear? *(train)*

Vroom, vroom, beep, beep, vroom!
What do I hear? *(car)*

Weeeoooo, weeeoooo, eeeooooeeeeooooo!
What do I hear? *(ambulance)*

Chop, chop, chka, chka, chop, chop!
What do I hear? *(helicopter)*

Zip, zoom, whoosh, voom!
What do I hear? *(airplane)*

IC2, IE5

266 Vacation: A Beanbag Rhyme

Give each child a beanbag to use during this rhyme.

I went to the train station to take a little vacation *(pass beanbag back and forth*
    between hands)
I went to the beach, *(move beanbag diagonally away from you, starting at your*
    right side, and ending up far out in front of you on your left side)
And then came home, *(bring beanbag back to right side)*
And had some relaxation. *(place beanbag into left hand)*

Repeat, replacing "the beach" with vacation destinations chosen by the children. Each time
you begin a new verse, you should be holding the beanbag in the hand opposite from the
previous verse. Make sure the diagonal cross-body movements also alternate hands between
verses. This simple motion of crossing the midline improves communication between the two
hemispheres of the brain.

IC2, IE5

267 Washing My Car

Pass out a small toy car and a baby wipe to each child. As you describe washing the car in
the story, encourage the children to wash their cars along with you.

On hot summer days, my mom and I wash our car. She says I am a great helper.
    First, I fill up the bucket with water *(mime filling bucket)*, squeeze in some soap
    (mime squeezing in soap), and mix it up until it's sudsy.
Then I take my rag—do you have yours? And I start washing! Let's wash the hood.
    Now the sides. Don't forget the tires! And the top . . . *(continue until the whole*
    car has been washed)
Then it's time to rinse off the soap with the hose! Mom hates it when I spray her
    instead! *(spray off imaginary car with a spray bottle, then spritz children)*
Next we dry off the car with a special cloth. *(pass out tissues and encourage the*
    children to dry off their cars with you)
Then it's time to drive the car around the block! *(form a line and let the children*
    drive their cars around the room)

IA1, IA2, IA3

268 Zorp's Spaceship

Preparation: Place four large, clear mixing bowls on a table. Turn one bowl over so that it presents a hard surface. Place a rubbery ball in the second bowl. Fill the third bowl with cotton balls and the fourth bowl with water. You will also need a small plastic or metal spaceship. If you don't have one, try making one from Legos.

Once there was an alien named Zorp. He loved zooming all over the galaxy in his spaceship. But he had to be careful, because the planets in his galaxy were a little wacky. In our world the planets are made up of rocks and gases, but his universe was different.

One day Zorp zoomed off in his spaceship, singing a little song. And he saw a really cool planet up ahead. It was hard and gleaming, almost like it was made of glass. He had to think really hard to make a prediction about what would happen when his ship hit the surface of the planet. What do you predict will happen? *(take answers from the children)*

Let's see! Zorp lowered his spaceship through the atmosphere, and *Boom!* The hard surface of the planet collided with his ship! It was damaged! But he worked and worked and fixed it up, and soon it could fly again.

Zorp took off again, looking for more planets. The next one he found had a rubbery kind of surface. What do you predict will happen when Zorp's ship tries to land on the rubbery planet? *(take answers from the children)*

Let's see! Zorp lowered his spaceship through the atmosphere, and *Boing!* His ship bounced off the rubbery surface of the planet! Off he went through the atmosphere.

"This is fun," said Zorp. "I wonder what kind of planet I will find next." Well, soon he saw a planet with a surface like soft, fluffy cotton balls. What do you predict will happen when Zorp's ship tries to land on the cotton ball planet? *(take answers from the children)*

Let's see! Zorp lowered his ship through the atmosphere and *Puff!* It slipped through the light cotton balls and below the surface. Zorp had to work the engines hard to find his way out of the fluffy cotton balls!

Zorp decided to explore one more planet. He saw this one, where the surface was covered in water. What do you predict will happen when Zorp's ship tries to land on the water planet? *(take answers from the children)*

Let's see! Zorp lowered his spaceship through the atmosphere, and *Splash!* Down it fell through the water. Zorp's ship was sinking!

"That's okay," said Zorp. And he pushed a few buttons, and his spaceship turned into a submarine. *Ping, ping, ping!*

Do you remember the kinds of planets that Zorp visited? What happened on each one? *(Have the children help you retell the story and their predictions for each planet; emphasize descriptive vocabulary such as soft, cottony, bouncy, hard, and wet.)*

IC2, IE1, IE3, IE5, IE6

More Entries Related to This Topic

Bookmobile, p. 140

Little Blue Truck Flannelboard, p. 81

*Truck Driver, Truck Driver Flannelboard, p. 128

Recommended Books

Train! by Judi Abbot. Wilton, CT: Tiger Tales, 2014.

Sputter, Sputter, Sput! by Babs Bell. New York: HarperCollins, 2008.

Hello Airplane! by Bill Cotter. Naperville, IL: Sourcebooks, 2014.

Five Trucks by Brian Floca. New York: Atheneum, 2014.

Red Truck by Kersten Hamilton. New York: Penguin, 2008.

Airplanes: Soaring! Turning! Diving! by Patricia Hubbell. Tarrytown, NY: Marshall Cavendish, 2008.

Watch Me Go! Sign Language for Vehicles by Dawn Babb Prochovnic. Edina, MN: Magic Wagon, 2010.

Sheep Blast Off! by Nancy Shaw. Boston: Houghton Mifflin, 2008.

Troto and the Trucks by Uri Shulevitz. New York: Farrar, Straus and Giroux, 2015.

Cars Galore by Peter Stein. Somerville, MA: Candlewick, 2011.

APPENDIX A
Further Resources for Storytime Planning

American Sign Language Clip and Create 5. Wheaton, MD: Institute for Disabilities Research and Training, Inc., 2005. www.idrt.com.

Baltuck, Naomi. *Crazy Gibberish and Other Story Hour Stretches*. Hamden, CT: Linnet Books, 1993.

Blythe, Sally Goddard. *The Well-Balanced Child: Movement and Early Learning*. Gloucestershire, UK: Hawthorn Press, 2006.

Briggs, Diane. *101 Fingerplays, Stories, and Songs to Use with Finger Puppets*. Chicago: American Library Association, 1999.

———. *Preschool Favorites: 35 Storytimes Kids Love*. Chicago: American Library Association, 2007.

Castellano, Marie. *Simply Super Storytimes: Programming Ideas for Ages 3–6*. Fort Atkinson, WI: Upstart Books, 2003.

Cullum, Carolyn N. *The Storytime Sourcebook: A Compendium of Ideas and Resources for Storytellers*. New York: Neal-Schuman, 1999.

———. *The Storytime Sourcebook II: A Compendium of 3,500+ New Ideas and Resources for Storytellers*. New York: Neal-Schuman, 2007.

Dennis, Kirsten, and Tressa Azpiri. *Sign to Learn: American Sign Language in the Early Childhood Classroom*. St. Paul, MN: Redleaf Press, 2005.

Diamant-Cohen, Betsy. *Mother Goose on the Loose*. Chicago: Neal-Schuman, 2006.

———. *Transforming Preschool Storytime: A Modern Vision and a Year of Programs*. Chicago: Neal-Schuman, 2013.

Dietzel-Glair, Julie. *Books in Motion: Connecting Preschoolers with Books through Art, Games, Movement, Music, Playacting, and Props*. Chicago: Neal-Schuman, 2013.

Faurot, Kimberly K. *Books in Bloom: Creative Patterns and Props That Bring Stories to Life*. Chicago: American Library Association, 2003.

———. *Storytime Around the Year*. Janesville, WI: Upstart Books, 2008.

Fujita, Hiroko. *Stories to Play With: Kids' Tales Told with Puppets, Paper, Toys, and Imagination*. Little Rock, AR: August House, 1999.

Ghoting, Saroj Nadkarni, and Pamela Martin-Diaz. *Storytimes for Everyone! Developing Young Children's Language and Literacy*. Chicago: American Library Association, 2013.

———. *Early Literacy Storytimes @ your library*. Chicago: American Library Association, 2006.

Ghoting, Saroj Nadkarni, and Kathy Fling Klatt. *STEP into Storytime: Using StoryTime Effective Practice to Strengthen the Development of Newborns to Five-Year-Olds*. Chicago: American Library Association, 2014.

Holt, David, and Bill Mooney, eds. *More Ready-to-Tell Tales from Around the World*. Little Rock, AR: August House, 2007.

MacDonald, Margaret Read. *Celebrate the World: Twenty Tellable Folktales for Multicultural Festivals*. New York: H. W. Wilson, 1994.

———. *Twenty Tellable Tales*. Chicago: American Library Association, 2005.

MacMillan, Kathy. *A Box Full of Tales: Easy Ways to Share Library Resources through Story Boxes*. Chicago: ALA Editions, 2008.

———. *Little Hands and Big Hands: Children and Adults Signing Together*. Chicago: Huron Street Press, 2013.

———. *Try Your Hand at This: Easy Ways to Incorporate Sign Language into Your Programs*. Lanham, MD: Scarecrow Press, 2006.

MacMillan, Kathy, and Christine Kirker. *Multicultural Storytime Magic*. Chicago: ALA Editions, 2012.

———. *Storytime Magic: 400 Fingerplays, Flannelboards, and Other Activities*. Chicago: ALA Editions, 2009.

McNeil, Heather. *Read, Rhyme, and Romp: Early Literacy Skills and Activities for Librarians, Teachers, and Parents*. Santa Barbara, CA: Libraries Unlimited, 2012.

Phelps, Joan Hilyer. *Book Tales*. Fort Atkinson, WI: Upstart Books, 2004.

Reid, Rob. *Children's Jukebox, Second Edition: The Select Subject Guide to Children's Musical Recordings*. Chicago: American Library Association, 2007.

———. *Family Storytime: Twenty-Four Creative Programs for All Ages*. Chicago: American Library Association, 1999.

———. *Storytime Slam! 15 Lesson Plans for Preschool and Primary Story Programs*. Fort Atkinson, WI: Upstart Books, 2006.

Schiller, Pam, and Jackie Silberg. *The Complete Book of Activities, Games, Stories, Props, Recipes, and Dances for Young Children*. Beltsville, MD: Gryphon House, 2003.

Silberg, Jackie, and Pam Schiller. *The Complete Book of Rhymes, Songs, Poems, Fingerplays, and Chants*. Beltsville, MD: Gryphon House, 2002.

Trevino, Rose Zertuche. *Read Me a Rhyme in Spanish and English*. Chicago: ALA Editions, 2009.

Common Core State Standards for Kindergarten

ALTHOUGH WE ARE aware of the controversial nature of the Common Core State Standards being implemented in many states, particularly in regard to early childhood education, we have chosen to include this appendix to assist educators and librarians who are required to justify the relationship of lesson or program content to benchmarks and standards. The following list includes the kindergarten standards for the Common Core State Standards, as preschool standards are not yet available. To learn more about the Common Core State Standards, see www.corestandards.org/read-the-standards.

Each entry in *More Storytime Magic* is coded to indicate which of the following standards it supports. Each code comprises the following elements:

A Roman numeral that indicates either broad section I for English Language Arts or II for Mathematics

A capital letter that indicates the subsection under the broad subject heading

An arabic number that indicates the specific standard under the subsection heading

For example, the code IA5 indicates the following standard:

I. English Language Arts Standards for Kindergarten

    A. Reading: Literature

        5. Recognize common types of texts.

I. ENGLISH LANGUAGE ARTS STANDARDS FOR KINDERGARTEN

A. Reading: Literature

1. With prompting and support, ask and answer questions about key details in a text.

2. With prompting and support, retell familiar stories, including key details.

3. With prompting and support, identify characters, settings, and major events in a story.

4. Ask and answer questions about unknown words in a text.

5. Recognize common types of texts.

6. With prompting and support, name the author and illustrator of a story and define the role of each in telling the story.

7. With prompting and support, describe the relationship between illustrations and the story in which they appear.

8. Not applicable to literature.

9. With prompting and support, compare and contrast the adventures and experiences of characters in familiar stories.

10. Actively engage in group reading activities with purpose and understanding.

B. Reading: Informational Text

1. With prompting and support, ask and answer questions about key details in a text.

2. With prompting and support, identify the main topic and retell key details of a text.

3. With prompting and support, describe the connection between two individuals, events, ideas, or pieces of information in a text.

4. With prompting and support, ask and answer questions about unknown words in a text.

5. Identify the front cover, back cover, and title page of a book.

6. Name the author and illustrator of a text and define the role of each in presenting the ideas or information in a text.

7. With prompting and support, describe the relationship between illustrations and the text in which they appear.

8. With prompting and support, identify the reasons an author gives to support points in a text.

9. With prompting and support, identify basic similarities in and differences between two texts on the same topic.

10. Actively engage in group reading activities with purpose and understanding.

C. Reading: Foundational Skills

1. Demonstrate understanding of the organization and basic features of print.

2. Demonstrate understanding of spoken words, syllables, and sounds (phonemes).

3. Know and apply grade-level phonics and word analysis skills in decoding words.

4. Read emergent-reader texts with purpose and understanding.

D. Writing

1. Use a combination of drawing, dictating, and writing to compose opinion pieces in which they tell a reader the topic or the name of the book they are writing about and state an opinion or preference about the topic or book.

2. Use a combination of drawing, dictating, and writing to compose informative/explanatory texts in which they name what they are writing about and supply some information about the topic.

3. Use a combination of drawing, dictating, and writing to narrate a single event or several loosely linked events, tell about the events in the order in which they occurred, and provide a reaction to what happened.

4. Does not apply to kindergarten.

5. With guidance and support from adults, respond to questions and suggestions from peers and add details to strengthen writing as needed.

6. With guidance and support from adults, explore a variety of digital tools to produce and publish writing, including in collaboration with peers.

7. Participate in shared research and writing projects.

8. With guidance and support from adults, recall information from experiences or gather information from provided sources to answer a question.

9. Does not apply to kindergarten.

10. Does not apply to kindergarten.

E. Speaking and Listening

1. Participate in collaborative conversations with diverse partners about kindergarten topics and texts with peers and adults in small and larger groups.

2. Confirm understanding of a text read aloud or information presented orally or through other media by asking and answering questions about key details and requesting clarification if something is not understood.

3. Ask and answer questions in order to seek help, get information, or clarify something that is not understood.

4. Describe familiar people, places, things, and events and, with prompting and support, provide additional detail.

5. Add drawings or other visual displays to descriptions as desired to provide additional detail.

6. Speak audibly and express thoughts, feelings, and ideas clearly.

F. Language

1. Demonstrate command of the conventions of standard English grammar and usage when writing or speaking.

2. Demonstrate command of the conventions of standard English capitalization, punctuation, and spelling when writing.

3. Does not apply to kindergarten.

4. Determine or clarify the meaning of unknown and multiple-meaning words and phrases based on kindergarten reading and content.

5. With guidance and support from adults, explore word relationships and nuances in word meanings.

6. Use words and phrases acquired through conversations, reading and being read to, and responding to texts.

II. MATHEMATICS

A. Counting and Cardinality

1. Count to 100 by ones and by tens.

2. Count forward beginning from a given number within the known sequence (instead of having to begin at 1).

3. Write numbers from 0 to 20.

4. Understand the relationship between numbers and quantities; connect counting to cardinality.

5. Count to answer "how many?" questions about as many as 20 things arranged in a line, a rectangular array, or a circle, or as many as 10 things in a scattered configuration; given a number from 1–20, count out that many objects.

6. Identify whether the number of objects in one group is greater than, less than, or equal to the number of objects in another group (e.g., by using matching and counting strategies).

7. Compare two numbers between 1 and 10 presented as written numerals.

B. Operations and Algebraic Thinking

1. Represent addition and subtraction with objects, fingers, mental images, drawings, sounds (e.g., claps), acting out situations, verbal explanations, expressions, or equations.

2. Solve addition and subtraction word problems, and add and subtract within 10 (e.g., by using objects or drawings to represent the problem).

3. Decompose numbers less than or equal to 10 into pairs in more than one way (e.g., by using objects or drawings), and record each decomposition by a drawing or equation (e.g., $5 = 2 + 3$ and $5 = 4 + 1$).

4. For any number from 1 to 9, find the number that makes 10 when added to the given number (e.g., by using objects or drawings), and record the answer with a drawing or equation.

5. Fluently add and subtract within 5.

C. Number and Operations in Base Ten

1. Compose and decompose numbers from 11 to 19 into ten ones and some further ones (e.g., by using objects or drawings), and record each composition or decomposition by a drawing or equation (such as $18 = 10 + 8$); understand that these numbers are composed of ten ones and one, two, three, four, five, six, seven, eight, or nine ones.

D. Measurement and Data

1. Describe measurable attributes of objects, such as length or weight. Describe several measurable attributes of a single object.
2. Directly compare two objects with a measurable attribute in common to see which object has "more of"/"less of" the attribute, and describe the difference.
3. Classify objects into given categories; count the numbers of objects in each category and sort the categories by count.

E. Geometry

1. Describe objects in the environment using names of shapes, and describe the relative positions of these objects using terms such as *above, below, beside, in front of, behind,* and *next to.*
2. Correctly name shapes regardless of their orientations or overall size.
3. Identify shapes as two-dimensional (lying in a plane, "flat") or three-dimensional ("solid").
4. Analyze and compare two- and three-dimensional shapes, in different sizes and orientations, using informal language to describe their similarities, differences, parts (e.g., number of sides and vertices/"corners"), and other attributes (e.g., having sides of equal length).
5. Model shapes in the world by building shapes from components (e.g., sticks and clay balls) and drawing shapes.
6. Compose simple shapes to form larger shapes.

Index